BLOOD

PHYSIOLOGY AND CIRCULATION

THE HUMAN BODY

BLOOD
PHYSIOLOGY AND CIRCULATION

EDITED BY KARA ROGERS, SENIOR EDITOR, BIOMEDICAL SCIENCES

Britannica®
Educational Publishing

IN ASSOCIATION WITH

ROSEN
EDUCATIONAL SERVICES

Published in 2011 by Britannica Educational Publishing
(a trademark of Encyclopædia Britannica, Inc.)
in association with Rosen Educational Services, LLC
29 East 21st Street, New York, NY 10010.

Distributed exclusively by Rosen Educational Services.
For a listing of additional Britannica Educational Publishing titles, call toll free (800) 237-9932.

First Edition

Britannica Educational Publishing
Michael I. Levy: Executive Editor
J.E. Luebering: Senior Manager
Marilyn L. Barton: Senior Coordinator, Production Control
Steven Bosco: Director, Editorial Technologies
Lisa S. Braucher: Senior Producer and Data Editor
Yvette Charboneau: Senior Copy Editor
Kathy Nakamura: Manager, Media Acquisition
Kara Rogers: Senior Editor, Biomedical Sciences

Rosen Educational Services
Jeanne Nagle: Senior Editor
Heather M. Moore Niver: Editor
Nelson Sá: Art Director
Cindy Reiman: Photography Manager
Matthew Cauli: Designer, Cover Design
Introduction by Don Rauf

Library of Congress Cataloging-in-Publication Data

Blood: physiology and circulation / edited by Kara Rogers.
    p. cm. — (The human body)
"In association with Britannica Educational Publishing, Rosen Educational Services."
Includes bibliographical references and index.
ISBN 978-1-61530-121-8 (library binding)
1. Blood—Popular works. 2. Blood—Circulation—Popular works. I. Rogers, Kara.
QP91.B6558 2010
612.1'15—dc22

                                                                    2010000145

CONTENTS

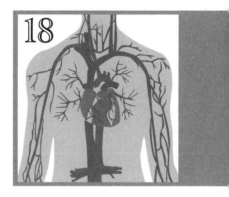

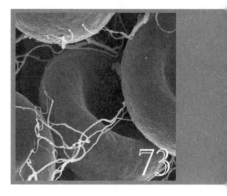

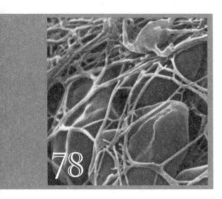

**CHAPTER 3: BLOOD GROUP
SYSTEMS 92**

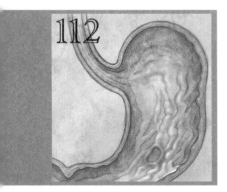

CHAPTER 4: BLOOD ANALYSIS AND THERAPEUTIC APPLICATIONS 121

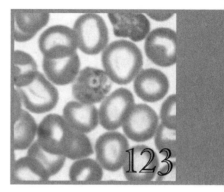

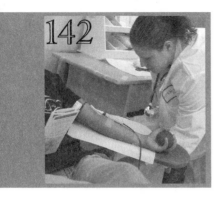

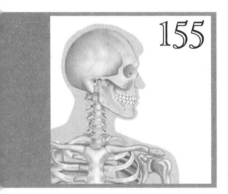

CHAPTER 5: DISEASES OF
RED BLOOD CELLS
AND HEMOGLOBIN 161

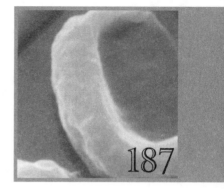

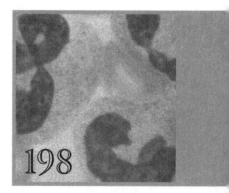

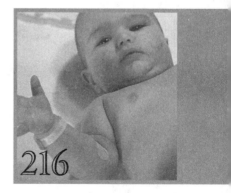

INTRODUCTION

Humans have been fascinated by the intricacies of blood as far back as early Egyptian civilization. Tombs in Egypt depicted bloodletting—a procedure through which blood is intentionally removed from a vein—as a treatment for sick patients. Some ancient Greeks drank the blood of a fallen warrior, believing that by doing so they would gain the dead man's strength and courage. Misunderstandings persisted for centuries. For instance, medical professionals still erroneously believed that bloodletting was the "cure" for a number of maladies well into the Common Era. It wasn't until 1628, when British physician William Harvey published his finding on how blood was pumped from the heart throughout the body and then recirculated, that the widespread practice of draining a person's blood was called into question.

A proper and thorough understanding of blood's function took thousands of years to develop. Throughout the 20th century and into the 21st, methods of examining, storing, and using blood were improved in order to more effectively fight disease and save lives. Indeed, the understanding of how blood works in the body has come a long way, as elucidated in this volume. Readers will discover virtually everything science has learned about blood, from its basic properties to its circulation through the body to its malfunction in disease.

Blood has numerous functions in a healthy body. One of its primary tasks is to deliver oxygen and nutrients to the body's cells. Blood also distributes warmth to those regions that need it the most, wards off disease, and helps to filter harmful waste products such as carbon dioxide out of the body.

The various components of blood each play a role. In humans, blood cells are produced by stem cells in the bone marrow. Once these cells develop, they are released into the bloodstream. Red blood cells deliver hemoglobin, which is the iron-bearing protein that makes the transportation of oxygen possible. Hemoglobin also gives human blood, and that of many other animals, its red colour. Certain creatures have different oxygen-carrying pigments, such as hemocyanin or chlorocruorin. When oxygenated, these pigments turn blood various colours; for example, blood is blue when the copper-rich hemocyanin is present, and it is green when chlorocruorin is present. The existence of different types of blood pigments explains why crustaceans such as lobsters have blue blood.

Also known as erythrocytes, red blood cells make up about 45 percent of blood. The liquid portion of the blood, plasma, makes up about 54 percent of blood's content. Although 90 percent water, plasma contains elements that are essential for sustaining health and life, including critical proteins. The remaining 1 percent of blood's composition is made up of white blood cells (leukocytes) and platelets (thrombocytes). White blood cells help protect the body from infections and disease by destroying the agents that cause illness. White blood cells are further categorized as lymphocytes, which help the body's immunity, and phagocytic cells (both granulocytes and monocytes), which ingest and break down microorganisms and foreign particles. The tiny fragments called platelets are important in the formation of blood clots (coagulation).

The average adult has about 5 quarts (4 to 5 litres) of blood coursing through his or her body, working in conjunction with organs to control concentrations of various elements necessary to keeping a person healthy. The lungs deliver oxygen, for example, and the kidneys take away extra water and waste. The liver performs several functions together with blood, including the removal of toxins, the manufacture of blood-clotting agents, and the destruction of old red blood cells. (The average red blood cell can survive as many as 120 days.) The liver also stores sugars, which are converted into glycogen. When the body needs energy, the glycogen is converted back to glucose and is released into the bloodstream.

The body depends on the circulatory system for blood to carry out its functions. The heart is the engine that keeps the bloodstream flowing, carrying blood away from the heart in arteries and transporting it back through veins.

Two veins, the inferior vena cava and the superior vena cava, allow blood to enter the heart's right chamber, while the aorta pumps blood out from the left chamber. Each beat of the heart involves both muscular relaxation, to let blood in, and muscular contraction, to push blood out. The average human heart beats about 60 to 80 times per minute, but it slows during sleep and beats faster during exercise.

Arteries transport blood away from the heart. First they feed into smaller vessels called arterioles and then into even tinier capillaries, which transport the blood to the body's tissues. The network of capillaries—each of which is smaller in diameter than a human hair and just large enough for red blood cells to pass through in single file—is extensive. The capillaries also connect to small veins called venules, which connect to veins for the blood's journey back to the heart.

The force that blood flow exerts against the walls of blood vessels is called blood pressure, and it is, in every sense, a true life force. Among the standard tests medical professionals perform to gauge a person's health is the measurement of his or her blood pressure. Two types of readings are taken: systolic, which is the force as the heart pumps blood out to the tissues, and diastolic, which is the pressure as the heart relaxes. Doctors give the measurement with a number indicating systolic pressure on top and diastolic pressure on the bottom. According to the

American Heart Association, a healthy blood pressure for an adult age 20 years or older is less than $^{120}/_{80}$. High blood pressure, which is called hypertension, can be a warning sign of developing heart disease, kidney disease, hardening of the arteries, and stroke. Proper diet and regular exercise can help keep blood pressure at healthy levels.

Blood volume is just as important to healthy body function as blood pressure. The body's self-defence measure against blood loss is hemostasis, a coagulation mechanism that forms a clot when blood vessels are damaged. When blood leaks from a vessel, cells release chemicals that give the platelets a sticky quality, which allows them to bond together and clot. Simultaneously, threads called fibrin are generated, which help trap more blood cells. A scab on a scraped knee is the handiwork of the blood's hemostasis mechanism. Vitamin K (from the Danish word *koagulation*) is required for the synthesis of several blood-clotting factors.

In a case when serious blood loss occurs, doctors have the option of performing a transfusion. The procedure of transferring blood from one person to another, which is called a blood transfusion, may be required to treat extensive hemorrhaging, burns, or trauma; to increase the number and concentration of red blood cells in persons with anemia; and to treat shock. Transfusion was made much safer in 1901, when American biologist Karl Landsteiner first identified blood by groups—A, B, AB, or O. Blood is typed according to the presence or absence of proteins called antigens on red cells. Blood group O, the most common in the world and known as the universal blood type, lacks A or B antigens.

Blood is also commonly identified by an antigen called the Rhesus (Rh) factor. In blood shorthand, presence of Rh is noted with a + (positive sign), and its absence is marked with a – (negative sign). For a successful transfusion, it is preferable to use a patient's exact blood type. Failing that, a compatible blood type needs to be found, but not all blood types are compatible. For example, a person who has type A blood can receive only types A and O blood because O is the universal blood type and can be transfused to people with other types of blood.

There are additional blood group systems, named for the presence or absence of certain, often rare, antigens. These systems include the P, MNSs, Kidd, Kell, Diego, Lutheran, Duffy, and Lewis systems. A Coombs test can help detect these antigens.

Doctors can use blood samples, often referred to as "blood work," to diagnose their patients. One of the most common blood tests, the complete blood count (CBC) test, is a broad screening exam that can detect disorders. Blood testing can also be used to diagnose allergies, auto-immune diseases, cancer, diabetes, gastrointestinal problems, kidney disease, and liver disease, as well as many other conditions.

Disease can also be contained within blood itself. There are disorders that affect red cells, compromising the blood's ability to deliver oxygen to bodily tissue and organs. The most common of these is anemia, which is a condition caused by there being too few or a low volume of red cells in a person's blood composition. Hemoglobin abnormalities are responsible for illnesses such as sickle cell anemia, where red cells exhibit a sickle-shaped deformity, and thalassemia, which is a group of blood disorders marked by hemoglobin deficiency.

Diseases of the white blood cells typically result in immune system suppression, making the body more susceptible to the negative effects of infections. Abnormalities in size, shape, and number of white blood cells are indicative of infections ranging from the relatively innocuous mononucleosis to life-threatening diseases such as leukemia.

Because bone marrow produces white blood cells, bone marrow transplants have been used to treat specific immune deficiency and hematological disorders.

Problems with coagulation define another category of blood disease. Bleeding disorders, which may be either inherited or acquired, are conditions that cause excessive or spontaneous bleeding in response to minor injury. The most readily recognizable of these diseases is hemophilia.

The American Red Cross reports that every two seconds someone in the United States is in need of blood. Blood from donors is essential to replace the blood lost in a patient who is undergoing a major operation, such as an organ transplant, that may involve copious blood loss. Through the 1940s, blood banks rapidly developed throughout the United States as the means to take blood from donors, and the ability to store blood improved. Blood can now be stored for up to 49 days with refrigeration and the addition of special preservatives. Advanced methods allow for the "fractioning" of blood when needed, separating the distinct components for specific treatments. For instance, chronic anemia can be treated with packed red blood, and white blood cells can be used to treat those who have a low white blood cell count and are battling infection. Platelets may be used for bleeding when there is a platelet deficiency. Because blood is capable of carrying disease, all donated blood is tested for HIV (human immunodeficiency virus), hepatitis B and C, and other infectious agents.

The human heart pumps a vast amount of precious blood each day—on average, nearly 600 pints per hour. Through this volume's provocative exploration of blood's properties and components, how it maintains the body, how it provides indication of disease and health, and how it can save lives, one can certainly understand why blood is called the fluid of life.

CHAPTER 1

THE FLUID OF LIFE

B lood is a fundamental component of human life. Within the adult body, approximately 4 to 5 litres (1 to 1.3 gallons) of blood circulates continuously through an intricate network of vessels, driven by the powerful contractions of the beating heart. As blood moves away from the lungs and heart, passing through large arteries and winding into increasingly narrower and more complex networks of small vessels, it comes into contact with the individual cells of tissues. At this level, its primary function is to feed these cells, delivering to them a multitude of nutrients, including oxygen—the most basic element necessary for human survival—which it has been carrying since its departure from the lungs. In exchange for these beneficial nutrients, blood picks up and carries away cellular wastes, such as carbon dioxide, that will ultimately be removed from the body as the blood travels back to the lungs.

The basic components of blood consist of specialized cells and fluids. Each of these components performs one or more well-defined functions physiologically, and each can be isolated and tested in a laboratory, thereby providing vital information about a person's health. Indeed, blood is one of the most easily accessed and readily examined tissues of the human body. Blood analysis has played a key role in the diagnosis of disease as well as the success of multiple lifesaving procedures, including blood transfusions and bone marrow transplantations. Although much is known about blood, it remains a subject of intense scientific investigation, fueled especially by the desire for an improved understanding of the role of white blood cells in pathological processes and in defense against infection.

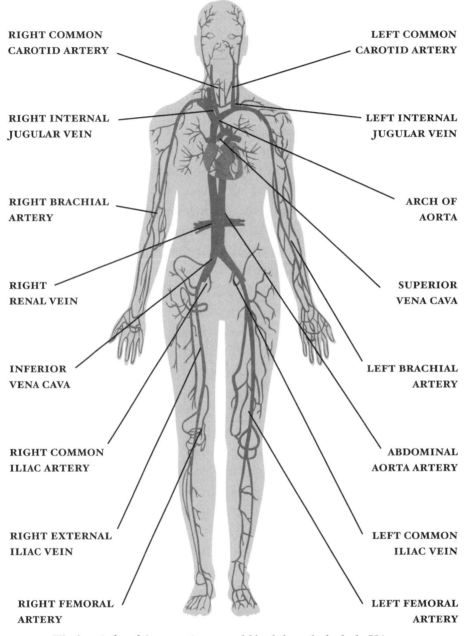

RIGHT COMMON
CAROTID ARTERY

LEFT COMMON
CAROTID ARTERY

RIGHT INTERNAL
JUGULAR VEIN

LEFT INTERNAL
JUGULAR VEIN

RIGHT BRACHIAL
ARTERY

ARCH OF
AORTA

RIGHT
RENAL VEIN

SUPERIOR
VENA CAVA

INFERIOR
VENA CAVA

LEFT BRACHIAL
ARTERY

RIGHT COMMON
ILIAC ARTERY

ABDOMINAL
AORTA ARTERY

RIGHT EXTERNAL
ILIAC VEIN

LEFT COMMON
ILIAC VEIN

RIGHT FEMORAL
ARTERY

LEFT FEMORAL
ARTERY

The heart's forceful contractions propel blood through the body. Veins carry blood to the heart and lungs, where oxygen is replenished before arteries pump it back through the body. Shutterstock.com

BLOOD

Technically, blood is a transport liquid pumped by the heart to all parts of the body, after which it is returned to the heart to repeat the process. Blood is both a tissue and a fluid. It is a tissue because it is a collection of similar specialized cells that serve particular functions. These cells are suspended in a liquid matrix (plasma), which makes the blood a fluid. If blood flow ceases, death will occur within minutes because of the effects of an unfavourable environment on highly susceptible cells.

The constancy of blood's composition is made possible by the circulation, which conveys blood through the organs that regulate the concentrations of its components. In the lungs, blood acquires oxygen and releases carbon dioxide transported from the tissues. The kidneys remove excess water and dissolved waste products. Nutrient substances derived from food reach the bloodstream after absorption by the gastrointestinal tract. Glands of the endocrine system release their secretions into the blood, which transports these hormones to the tissues in which they exert their effects. Many substances are recycled through the blood. For example, iron released during the destruction of old red cells is conveyed by the plasma to sites of new red cell production where it is reused. Each of blood's numerous components is kept within appropriate concentration limits by an effective regulatory mechanism. In many instances, feedback control systems are operative. Thus, a declining level of blood sugar (glucose) leads to accelerated release of glucose into the blood so that a potentially hazardous depletion of glucose does not occur.

Unicellular organisms, primitive multicellular animals, and the early embryos of higher forms of life lack a circulatory system. Because of their small size, these organisms can absorb oxygen and nutrients, as well as discharge wastes, directly into their surrounding medium by simple diffusion. Sponges and coelenterates (e.g., jellyfish and hydras) also lack a blood system, so the means to transport foodstuffs and oxygen to all the cells of these larger multicellular animals is provided by water, sea or fresh, pumped through spaces inside the organisms. In larger and more complex animals, transport of adequate amounts of oxygen and other substances requires some type of blood circulation. In most such animals, the blood passes through a respiratory exchange membrane, which lies in the gills, lungs, or even the skin. There the blood picks up oxygen and disposes of carbon dioxide.

The cellular composition of blood varies from group to group in the animal kingdom. Most invertebrates have various large blood cells capable of amoeboid movement, some of which aid in transporting substances while other are capable of surrounding and digesting foreign particles or debris (phagocytosis). Compared with vertebrate blood, however, that of the invertebrates has relatively few cells. Among the vertebrates, there are several classes of amoeboid cells (white blood cells, or leukocytes) and cells that help stop bleeding (platelets, or thrombocytes).

Oxygen requirements have played a major role in determining both the composition of blood and the architecture of the circulatory system. In some simple animals, including small worms and mollusks, transported oxygen is merely dissolved in the plasma. Larger and more complex animals, which have greater oxygen needs, have pigments capable of transporting relatively large amounts of oxygen. The red pigment hemoglobin, which contains iron, is found in all vertebrates and in some invertebrates. In almost all vertebrates, including humans, hemoglobin is contained exclusively within the red blood cells (erythrocytes). The red cells of the lower vertebrates (e.g., birds) have a nucleus, whereas mammalian red cells lack a nucleus. Red cells vary markedly in size among mammals. For example, those of the goat are much smaller than those of humans, but the goat compensates by having many more red cells per unit volume of blood. The concentration of hemoglobin inside the red cell varies little between species. Hemocyanin, a copper-containing protein chemically unlike hemoglobin, is found in some crustaceans. Hemocyanin is blue in colour when oxygenated and colourless when oxygen is removed. Some annelids have the iron-containing green pigment chlorocruorin, whereas others have the iron-containing red pigment hemerythrin. In many invertebrates the respiratory pigments are carried in solution in the plasma, but in higher animals, including all vertebrates, the pigments are enclosed in cells. If the pigments were freely in solution, the pigment concentrations required would cause the blood to be so viscous as to impede circulation.

BLOOD COMPONENTS

In humans, blood is an opaque red fluid, freely flowing but denser and more viscous than water. The characteristic colour is imparted by hemoglobin, a unique iron-containing protein. Hemoglobin brightens in colour when saturated with oxygen (oxyhemoglobin) and darkens when oxygen is removed (deoxyhemoglobin). For this reason, the partially deoxygenated blood from a vein is darker than oxygenated blood from an artery. The red blood cells constitute about 45 percent of the volume of the blood, and the remaining cells (white blood cells and platelets) less than 1 percent. The fluid portion, plasma, is a clear, slightly sticky, yellowish liquid. After a fatty meal, plasma transiently appears turbid. Within the body the blood is

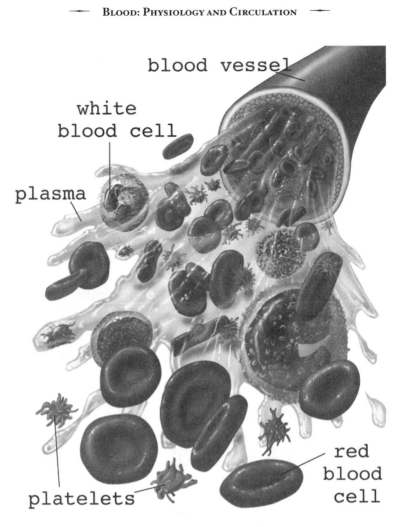

Blood is made up of multiple components, including red blood cells, white blood cells, platelets, and plasma. Encyclopædia Britannica, Inc.

permanently fluid, and turbulent flow assures that cells and plasma are fairly homogeneously mixed.

The total amount of blood in humans varies with age, sex, weight, body type, and other factors, but a rough average figure for adults is about 60 to 65 ml per kg (about 1 ounce per 1.2 pounds) of body weight. This figure can be broken down into plasma volume and red cell volume.

Thus, a young male may have a plasma volume of about 35 ml per kg (0.6 ounce per 1.2 pounds) and a red cell volume of about 30 ml per kg (0.5 ounce per 1.2 pounds) of body weight. There is little variation in the blood volume of a healthy person over long periods, although each component of the blood is in a continuous state of flux. In particular, water rapidly moves in and out of the bloodstream, achieving a balance with the extravascular fluids (those outside the blood vessels) within minutes.

The normal volume of blood provides such an adequate reserve that appreciable blood loss is well tolerated. Withdrawing 500 ml (about 1 pint) of blood from normal blood donors is a harmless procedure, because blood volume is rapidly replaced after blood loss. Within hours, plasma volume is restored by movement of extravascular fluid into the circulation. Red cells are completely replaced within several weeks. The vast area of capillary membrane, through which water passes freely, would permit instantaneous loss of the plasma from the circulation were it not for the plasma proteins—in particular, serum albumin. Capillary membranes are impermeable to serum albumin, the smallest in weight and highest in concentration of the plasma proteins. The osmotic effect of serum albumin retains fluid within the circulation, opposing the hydrostatic forces that tend to drive the fluid outward into the tissues.

PLASMA

The liquid portion of the blood, the plasma, is a complex solution containing more than 90 percent water. Plasma serves as a transport medium for delivering nutrients to the cells of the various organs of the body and for transporting waste products derived from cellular metabolism to the kidneys, liver, and lungs for excretion. It is also a transport system for blood cells, and it plays a critical role in maintaining normal blood pressure. Plasma helps to distribute heat throughout the body and to maintain homeostasis, or biological stability, including acid-base balance in the blood and body. The water of the plasma is freely exchangeable with that of body cells and other extracellular fluids and is available to maintain the normal state of hydration of all tissues. Water, the single largest constituent of the body, is essential to the existence of every living cell.

Of all the constituents of plasma, the proteins are the most abundant, making up about 7 percent of the plasma by weight. In fact, the principal difference between the plasma and the extracellular fluid of the tissues is the high protein content of the plasma. Plasma protein exerts an osmotic effect by which water tends to move from other extracellular fluid to the plasma. When dietary protein is digested in the gastrointestinal tract, individual amino acids are released from the polypeptide chains and absorbed. The amino acids are transported through the plasma to all parts of the body, where they are taken up by cells and assembled in specific ways to form proteins of many types. These plasma proteins are released into the blood from the cells in which they were synthesized. Much of the protein of plasma is produced in the liver.

The major plasma protein is serum albumin, a relatively small molecule synthesized in the liver, the principal function of which is to retain water in the bloodstream by its osmotic effect. Serum albumin constitutes approximately 60 percent of all of the plasma proteins. The amount of serum albumin in the blood is a determinant of the total volume of plasma. Depletion of serum albumin permits fluid to leave the circulation and to accumulate and cause swelling of soft tissues (edema). Serum albumin binds certain other substances that are transported in plasma and thus serves as a nonspecific carrier protein. Bilirubin, for example, is bound to serum albumin during its passage through the blood. Serum albumin has physical properties that permit its separation from other plasma proteins, which as a group are called globulins. In fact, the globulins are a heterogeneous array of proteins of widely varying structure and function, only a few of which will be mentioned here. The immunoglobulins, or antibodies, are an important class of proteins that are secreted by cells of the immune system known as B cells (or B lymphocytes). The immunoglobulins provide most of the body's supply of protective antibodies and are produced in response to a specific foreign substance, or antigen. For example, administration of polio vaccine, which is made from killed or attenuated (weakened) poliovirus, is followed by the appearance in the plasma of antibodies that react with poliovirus and effectively prevent the onset of disease. Antibodies may be induced by many foreign substances in addition to microorganisms; immunoglobulins are involved in some hypersensitivity and allergic reactions.

Another group of molecules found in the plasma consists of small, short-lived proteins called cytokines, which are synthesized by cells of various organs and by cells found in the immune system and bone marrow. They serve as intercellular chemical messengers that regulate blood cell formation (hematopoiesis), though they are perhaps best known for the roles they play in the immune system's defense against disease-causing organisms. One cytokine called erythropoietin, synthesized by specialized kidney cells, stimulates bone marrow blood progenitor cells to produce red blood cells. Other cytokines stimulate the production of white blood cells and platelets. Another protein system in the plasma, called complement, is important in mediating appropriate immune and inflammatory responses to a variety of infectious agents.

Many proteins are involved in highly specific ways with the transport function of the blood. Blood lipids are incorporated into protein molecules as lipoproteins, substances important in lipid transport. Iron and copper are transported in plasma by unique metal-binding proteins (transferrin and ceruloplasmin, respectively). Proteins called alpha and beta globulins transport lipids such as cholesterol as well as steroids and sugar. Vitamin B_{12}, an essential nutrient, is bound to a specific carrier protein. Although hemoglobin is not normally released into the plasma, a hemoglobin-binding protein (haptoglobin) is available to transport hemoglobin to the reticuloendothelial system should hemolysis (breakdown) of red cells occur. The serum haptoglobin level is raised during inflammation and certain other conditions; it is lowered in hemolytic disease and some types of liver disease.

Another critical group of plasma proteins is the coagulation proteins and their inhibitors, synthesized primarily in the liver. When blood clotting is activated, fibrinogen circulating in the blood is converted to fibrin, which in turn helps to form a stable blood clot at the site of vascular disruption. Coagulation inhibitor proteins help to prevent abnormal coagulation (hypercoagulability) and to resolve clots after they are formed.

Lipids are present in plasma in suspension and in solution. The concentration of lipids in plasma varies, particularly in relation to meals, but ordinarily does not exceed 1 gram per 100 ml. The largest fraction consists of phospholipids, complex molecules containing phosphoric acid and a nitrogen base in addition to fatty acids and glycerol. Triglycerides, or simple fats, are molecules composed only of fatty acids and glycerol. Free fatty acids, lower in concentration than triglycerides, are responsible for a much larger transport of fat. Other lipids include cholesterol, a major fraction of the total plasma lipids. These substances exist in plasma combined with proteins of several types as lipoproteins. The largest lipid particles in the blood are known as chylomicrons and consist largely of triglycerides; after absorption from the intestine, they pass through lymphatic channels and enter the blood-stream through the thoracic lymph duct. The other plasma lipids are derived from food or enter the plasma from tissue sites.

Some plasma constituents occur in plasma in low concentration but have a high turnover rate and great physiological importance. Among these is glucose, or blood sugar. Glucose is absorbed from the gastrointestinal tract or may be released into the circulation from the liver. It provides a source of energy for tissue cells and is the only source of energy for some cells, including the red cells. Glucose is conserved and used and is not normally excreted. Amino acids also are so rapidly transported that the plasma level remains low, but they are required for all protein synthesis throughout the body. Urea, an end product of protein metabolism, is rapidly excreted by the kidneys. Other nitrogenous waste products, such as uric acid and creatinine, are similarly removed.

Several inorganic materials are essential constituents of plasma, and each has special functional attributes. The predominant cation (positively charged ion) of the plasma is sodium, an ion that occurs within cells at a much lower concentration. Because of the effect of sodium on osmotic pressure and fluid movements, the amount of sodium in the body is an influential determinant of the total volume of extracellular fluid. The amount of sodium in plasma is controlled by the kidneys under the influence of the hormone aldosterone, which is secreted by the adrenal gland. If dietary sodium exceeds requirements, the excess is excreted by the kidneys. Potassium, the principal intra-cellular cation, occurs in plasma at a much lower concentration than sodium. The renal excretion of potassium is influenced by aldosterone, which causes retention of sodium and loss of potassium. Calcium in plasma is in part bound to protein and in part ionized. Its concentration is under the control of two hormones: parathyroid hormone (or parathormone), which causes the level to rise, and calcitonin, which causes it to fall. Magnesium, similar to potassium, is a predominantly intracellular cation and occurs in plasma in low concentration. Variations in the concentrations of these cations may have profound effects on the nervous system, the muscles, and the heart, effects normally prevented by precise regulatory mechanisms. Although iron, copper, and zinc are required in trace amounts for synthesis of essential enzymes, much more iron is needed in addition for production of hemoglobin and myoglobin, the oxygen-binding pigment of muscles. These metals occur in plasma in low concentrations. The principal anion (negatively charged ion) of plasma is chloride, and sodium chloride is its major salt. Bicarbonate participates in the transport of carbon dioxide and in the regulation of pH. Phosphate also has a buffering effect on the pH of the blood and is vital for chemical reactions of cells and for the metabolism of calcium. Transported through plasma in trace amounts, iodide is avidly taken up by the thyroid gland, which incorporates it into thyroid hormone.

The hormones of all the endocrine glands are secreted into the plasma and transported to their target organs, the organs on which they exert their effects. The plasma levels of these agents often reflect the functional activity of the glands that secrete them. In some instances, measurements are possible when concentrations are extremely low. Among the many other constituents of plasma are numerous enzymes, some of which appear simply to have escaped from tissue cells and have no functional significance in the blood.

BLOOD CELLS

There are four major types of blood cells: red blood cells, platelets (thrombocytes), lymphocytes, and phagocytic cells. Collectively, the lymphocytes and phagocytic cells constitute the white blood cells. Each type of blood cell has a specialized function: red cells take up oxygen from the lungs and deliver it to the tissues; platelets participate in forming blood clots; lymphocytes are involved with immunity; and phagocytic cells occur in two varieties—granulocytes and monocytes—and ingest and break down microorganisms and foreign particles. The circulating blood functions as a conduit, bringing the various kinds of cells to the regions of the body where they are needed: red cells to tissues requiring oxygen, platelets to sites of injury, lymphocytes to areas of infection, and phagocytic cells to sites of microbial invasion and inflammation.

The continuous process of blood cell formation (hematopoiesis) takes place in hematopoietic tissue. In the developing embryo, the first site of blood formation is the yolk sac. Later in embryonic life, the liver becomes the most important red blood cell-forming organ, but it is soon succeeded by the bone marrow, which in adult life is the only source of both red cells and the granulocytes. In young children, hematopoietic bone marrow fills most of the skeleton, whereas in adults the marrow is located mainly in the central bones (ribs, sternum, vertebrae, and pelvic bones). Bone marrow is a rich mixture of developing and mature blood cells, as well as fat cells and other cells that provide nutrition and an architectural framework upon which the blood-forming elements arrange themselves. The weight of the marrow of a normal adult is 1,600 to 3,700 grams and contains more than 1,000,000,000,000 hematopoietic cells (18×10^9 cells per kg). Nourishment of this large mass of cells comes from the blood itself. Arteries pierce the outer walls of the bones, enter the marrow, and divide into fine branches, which ultimately coalesce into large venous sacs (sinusoids) through which blood sluggishly flows. In the surrounding hematopoietic tissue, newly formed blood cells enter the general circulation by penetrating the walls of the sinusoids.

In the adult, the bone marrow produces all the red cells, 60 to 70 percent of the white cells (i.e., the granulocytes), and all the platelets. The lymphatic tissues, particularly the thymus, the spleen, and the lymph nodes, produce the lymphocytes (comprising 20 to 30 percent of the white cells). The reticuloendothelial tissues of the spleen, liver, lymph nodes, and other organs produce the monocytes (4 to 8 percent of the white cells). The platelets are formed from bits of the cytoplasm of the giant cells (megakaryocytes) of the bone marrow.

Both the red and white cells arise through a series of complex transformations from primitive stem cells, which have the ability to form any of the precursors of a blood cell. Precursor cells are stem cells that have developed to the stage where they are committed to forming a particular type of new blood cell. By dividing and differentiating, precursor cells give rise to the four major blood cell lineages: red cells, phagocytic cells, megakaryocytes, and lymphocytes. The cells of the marrow are under complex controls that regulate their formation and adjust their production to the changing demands of the body. When marrow stem cells are cultured outside the body, they form tiny clusters of cells (colonies), which correspond to red cells, phagocytic cells, and megakaryocytes. The formation of these individual colonies depends on hormonal sugar-containing proteins (glycoproteins), referred to collectively as colony-stimulating factors (CSFs). These factors are produced throughout the body. Even in minute amounts, CSFs can stimulate the division and differentiation of precursor cells into mature blood cells and thus exert powerful regulatory influences over the production of blood cells. A master colony-stimulating factor (multi-CSF), also called interleukin-3, stimulates the most ancestral hematopoietic stem cell.

Further differentiation of this stem cell into specialized descendants requires particular kinds of CSFs; for example, the CSF erythropoietin is needed for the maturation of red cells, and granulocyte CSF controls the production of granulocytes. These glycoproteins, as well as other CSFs, serve as signals from the tissues to the marrow. For instance, a decrease in the oxygen content of the blood stimulates the kidney to increase its production of erythropoietin, thus ultimately raising the number of oxygen-carrying red cells. Certain bacterial components accelerate the formation of granulocyte CSF, thereby leading to an increased production of phagocytic granulocytes by the bone marrow during infection.

In the normal adult, the rate of blood cell formation varies depending on the individual. A typical production might average 200 billion red cells per day, 10 billion white cells per day, and 400 billion platelets per day.

Red Blood Cells

The millions of red blood cells that occur in the circulation of vertebrates give the blood its characteristic colour. The function of the red cell and its hemoglobin is to carry oxygen from the lungs to all the body tissues and to transport carbon dioxide, a waste product of metabolism, to the lungs, where it is excreted.

The red blood cells are highly specialized, well adapted for their primary function of oxygen transport. This adaptation is made evident by several important features of the cells. Oxygen-carrying pigment is concentrated in red cells in vertebrates, and thus oxygen and carbon dioxide are efficiently exchanged as gases. This represents an important evolutionary development relative to invertebrates, in which the pigment circulates freely, not contained within cells. The mammalian red cell is further adapted by lacking a nucleus—the amount of oxygen required by the cell for its own metabolism is thus very low, and most oxygen carried can be freed into the tissues. The biconcave shape of the cell allows oxygen exchange at a constant rate over the largest possible area, because it provides a large surface-to-volume ratio.

The red blood cell is surrounded by a thin membrane that is composed of chemically complex lipids, proteins, and carbohydrates in a highly organized structure. The mature human red cell, which is small (approximately 7.8

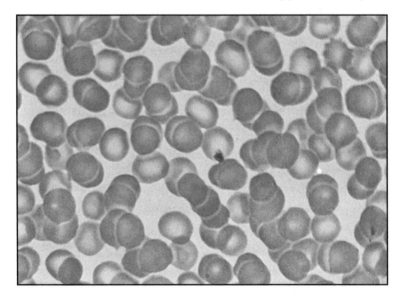

Human red blood cells (erythrocytes). Manfred Kage—Peter Arnold

micrometres in diameter [a micrometre is 0.001 mm]), is extremely flexible and experiences extraordinary distortion in its passage through minute blood vessels, many of which have a diameter less than that of the red cell. When the deforming stress is removed, the cell springs back to its original shape. The red cell readily tolerates bending and folding, but, if appreciable stretching of the membrane occurs, the cell is damaged or destroyed. The membrane is freely permeable to water, oxygen, carbon dioxide, glucose, urea, and certain other substances, but it is impermeable to hemoglobin. Within the cell the major cation is potassium, whereas in plasma and extracellular fluids the major cation is sodium. A pumping mechanism, driven by enzymes within the red cell, maintains its sodium and potassium concentrations. Red cells are also subject to osmotic effects. When they are suspended in very dilute (hypotonic) solutions of sodium chloride, red cells take in water, which causes them to increase in volume and to become more spheroid. In concentrated salt solutions, they lose water and shrink.

The red blood cell develops in bone marrow in several stages. From a hemocytoblast, a multipotential cell in the mesenchyme, it becomes an erythroblast (normoblast). During two to five days of development, the erythroblast gradually fills with hemoglobin, and its nucleus and mitochondria (particles in the cytoplasm that provide energy for the cell) disappear. In a late stage, the cell is called a reticulocyte, which ultimately becomes a fully mature red blood cell. The average red cell in humans lives 100 to 120 days.

When fresh blood is examined with the microscope, red cells appear to be yellow-green disks with pale centres containing no visible internal structures. When blood is centrifuged to cause the cells to settle, the volume of packed red cells (hematocrit value) ranges between 42 and

54 percent of total volume in men and between 37 and 47 percent in women, with values somewhat lower in children. Normal red blood cells are fairly uniform in volume, so the hematocrit value is determined largely by the number of red cells per unit of blood. The normal red cell count ranges between four million and six million per cubic millimetre.

When red cell membranes are damaged, hemoglobin and other dissolved contents may escape from the cells, leaving the membranous structures as "ghosts." This process, called hemolysis, is produced not only by the osmotic effects of water but also by numerous other mechanisms. These include physical damage to red cells, as when blood is heated, is forced under great pressure through a small needle, or is subjected to freezing and thawing; chemical damage to red cells by agents such as bile salts, detergents, and certain snake venoms; and damage caused by immunologic reactions that may occur when antibodies attach to red cells in the presence of complement. When such destruction proceeds at a greater than normal rate, hemolytic anemia results.

The membrane of the red cell has on its surface a group of molecules that confer blood group specificity (i.e., that differentiate blood cells into groups). Most blood group substances are composed of carbohydrate linked to protein, and it is usually the chemical structure of the carbohydrate portion that determines the specific blood type. Blood group substances are antigens capable of inducing the production of antibodies when injected into persons lacking the antigen. Detection and recognition of the blood group antigens are accomplished by the use of blood serum containing these antibodies. The large number of different red cell antigens makes it extremely unlikely that persons other than identical twins will have the same array of blood group substances.

Although red cells are usually round, a small proportion are oval in the normal person, and in certain hereditary states a higher proportion may be oval. Some diseases also display red cells of abnormal shape. For example, they may be oval in pernicious anemia, be crescent-shaped in sickle cell anemia, and have projections giving a thorny appearance in the hereditary disorder acanthocytosis. The number of red cells and the amount of hemoglobin vary among different individuals and under different conditions; the number is higher, for example, in persons who live at high altitudes and in the disease polycythemia. At birth the red cell count is high, falling shortly after birth and gradually rising to the adult level at puberty.

Hemoglobin

Hemoglobin is the iron-containing protein found in the red blood cells that transports oxygen to the tissues. Hemoglobin forms an unstable, reversible bond with oxygen. In the oxygenated state, it is called oxyhemoglobin and is bright red, and in the reduced state, it is purplish blue and may be referred to as deoxyhemoglobin.

Hemoglobin develops in bone marrow, specifically in the cells that become red blood cells. About 95 percent of the dry weight of the red cell consists of hemoglobin. When red cells die, hemoglobin is broken up. Iron is salvaged, transported to the bone marrow by proteins called transferrins, and used again in the production of new red blood cells. The remainder of the hemoglobin forms the basis of bilirubin, a chemical that is excreted into the bile and gives the feces their characteristic yellow-brown colour.

Each hemoglobin molecule has a tetrahedral structure. A hemoglobin protein assumes this structure because it contains four polypeptide chains (a tetramer), each chain consisting of more than 140 amino acids. To each chain is attached a chemical structure known as a heme

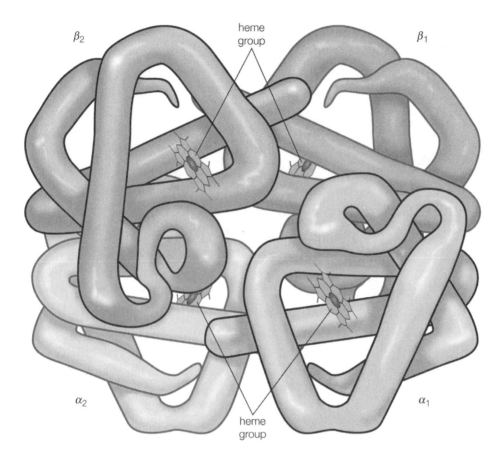

Artist's conception of the hemoglobin tetramer. Two αβ dimers combine to form the complete hemoglobin molecule. Each heme group contains a central iron atom, which is available to bind a molecule of oxygen. The α1β2 region is the area where the α₁ subunit interacts with the β2 subunit. Encyclopædia Britannica, Inc.

group. Heme accounts for about 4 percent of the weight of hemoglobin and is composed of a ringlike organic compound known as a porphyrin, to which an iron atom is attached. It is the iron atom that reversibly binds oxygen as the blood travels between the lungs and the tissues. There are four iron atoms in each molecule of hemoglobin, which, accordingly, can bind four atoms of oxygen. The complex porphyrin and protein structure provides the proper environment for the iron atom so that it binds and releases oxygen appropriately under physiological conditions.

The affinity of hemoglobin for oxygen is so great that at the oxygen pressure in the lungs about 95 percent of the hemoglobin is saturated with oxygen. As the oxygen tension falls, as it does in the tissues, oxygen dissociates from hemoglobin and is available to move by diffusion through the red cell membrane and the plasma to sites where it is used. The proportion of hemoglobin saturated with oxygen is not directly proportional to the oxygen pressure. As the oxygen pressure declines, hemoglobin gives up its oxygen with disproportionate rapidity, so that the major fraction of the oxygen can be released with a relatively small drop in oxygen tension. The affinity of hemoglobin for oxygen is primarily determined by the structure of hemoglobin, but it is also influenced by other conditions within the red cell, in particular the pH and certain organic phosphate compounds produced during the chemical breakdown of glucose, especially 2,3-diphosphoglycerate.

Hemoglobin has a much higher affinity for carbon monoxide than for oxygen. Carbon monoxide produces its lethal effects by binding to hemoglobin and preventing oxygen transport. The oxygen-carrying function of hemoglobin can be disturbed in other ways. The iron of hemoglobin is normally in the reduced or ferrous state, in both oxyhemoglobin and deoxyhemoglobin. If the iron becomes oxidized to the ferric state, hemoglobin is changed to methemoglobin, a brown pigment incapable of transporting oxygen. The red cells contain enzymes capable of maintaining the iron in its normal state, but under abnormal conditions large amounts of methemoglobin may appear in the blood.

Hemoglobin S is a variant form of hemoglobin that is present in persons who have sickle cell anemia, a serious and often fatal hereditary disease in which the red cells become crescent shaped when oxygen is lacking. Persons who have sickle cell anemia are predominantly of African descent. The disease is caused by the mutation of a single gene that determines the structure of the hemoglobin molecule. Sickle hemoglobin differs from normal hemoglobin in that a single amino acid (glutamic acid) in one pair of the polypeptide chains has been replaced by another (valine). This single intramolecular change so alters the properties of the hemoglobin molecule that anemia and other effects are produced. Many other genetically determined abnormalities of hemoglobin have been identified, some of which also produce several types. Study of the effects of altered structure of hemoglobin on its properties has greatly broadened knowledge of the structure-function relationships of the hemoglobin molecule.

Porphyrin

Porphyrins are water-soluble, nitrogenous biological pigments (biochromes). Derivatives of porphyrins include the hemoproteins (porphyrins combined with metals and protein), examples of which are the green, photosynthetic chlorophylls of higher plants; the hemoglobins in the blood of many animals; the cytochromes, enzymes that occur in minute quantities in most cells and are involved in oxidative processes; and catalase, also a widely distributed enzyme that accelerates the breakdown of hydrogen peroxide.

Porphyrins have complex cyclic structures. All porphyrin compounds absorb light intensely at or close to 410 nanometres. Structurally, porphyrin consists of four pyrrole rings (five-membered closed structures containing one nitrogen and four carbon atoms) linked to each other by methine groups (-CH=). The iron atom is kept in the centre of the porphyrin ring by interaction with the four nitrogen atoms. The iron atom can combine with two other substituents: in oxyhemoglobin one substituent is a histidine of the protein carrier and the other is an oxygen molecule. In some heme proteins, the protein is also bound covalently to the side chains of porphyrin.

Green chromoproteins called biliproteins are found in many insects, such as grasshoppers, and also in the egg-shells of many birds. The biliproteins are derived from the bile pigment biliverdin, which in turn is formed from porphyrin. Biliverdin contains four pyrrole rings and three of the four methine groups of porphyrin. Large amounts of biliproteins, the molecular weights of which are about 270,000, have been found in red algae (phycoerythrin) and blue-green algae (phycocyanobilin). Phycocyanobilin consists of eight subunits with a molecular weight of 28,000 each; about 89 percent of the molecule is protein with a large amount of carbohydrate.

Evidence indicates that in various animals certain porphyrins may be involved in activating hormones from the pituitary gland of the brain, including those concerned with the period of sexual heat in certain female animals. Porphyrins in the integument (skin) of some mollusks and cnidarians are regarded as being photosensitive receptors of light.

White Blood Cells

White blood cells (or leukocytes, sometimes called white corpuscles), unlike red cells, are nucleated, independently motile, and lack hemoglobin. They serve primarily to defend the body against infection and disease by ingesting foreign materials and cellular debris, destroying infectious agents and cancer cells, or producing antibodies. They also have some reparative functions. White cells are highly differentiated for their specialized functions. They do not undergo cell division (mitosis) in the bloodstream, however, some retain the capability of mitosis.

The number of white cells in normal blood ranges between 4,500 and 11,000 per cubic millimetre. Fluctuations occur during the day: lower values are obtained during rest and higher values during exercise. Intense physical exertion may cause the count to exceed 20,000 per cubic millimetre. White cell count also may increase in response to convulsions, strong emotional reactions, pain, pregnancy, labour, and certain disease states. Although white cells are found in the circulation, most occur outside the circulation; the few in the bloodstream are in transit from one site to another. As living cells, their survival depends on their continuous production of energy. The chemical pathways utilized are more complex than those of the red cells and are similar to those of other tissue cells. White cells, containing a nucleus and able to produce ribonucleic acid (RNA), can synthesize protein. On the basis of their appearance under a light microscope, white cells are grouped into three major classes—lymphocytes, granulocytes, and monocytes—each of which carries out somewhat different functions.

Lymphocytes, which are further divided into B and T cells, are responsible for the specific recognition of foreign agents and their subsequent removal from the host. B cells secrete antibodies, which are proteins that bind to foreign microorganisms in body tissues and mediate their destruction. Typically, T cells recognize virally infected or cancerous cells and destroy them, or they serve as helper cells to assist the production of antibody by B cells. Also included in this group are natural killer (NK) cells, so named for their inherent ability to kill a variety of target

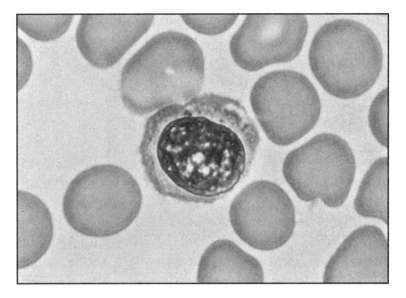

Human lymphocyte (phase-contrast microphotograph). Manfred Kage/ Peter Arnold

cells. In a healthy person, about 25 to 33 percent of white blood cells are lymphocytes.

The most numerous of the white cells, granulocytes rid the body of large pathogenic organisms such as protozoans or helminths and are also key mediators of allergy and other forms of inflammation. These cells contain many cytoplasmic granules. On the basis of how the granules take up dye in the laboratory, granulocytes are subdivided into three categories: neutrophils, eosinophils, and basophils. The most numerous of the granulocytes are neutrophils. They are often one of the first cell types to arrive at a site of infection, where they engulf and destroy the infectious microorganisms through a process called phagocytosis. Eosinophils and basophils, as well as the tissue cells called mast cells, typically arrive later. The granules of basophils and of the closely related mast cells contain a number of chemicals, including histamine and leukotrienes, that are important in inducing allergic inflammatory responses. Eosinophils destroy parasites and also help modulate inflammatory responses.

Constituting between 4 and 8 percent of the total number of white cells in the blood, monocytes move from the blood to sites of infection, where they differentiate further into macrophages. These cells are scavengers that phagocytose whole or killed microorganisms and are therefore effective at direct destruction of pathogens and cleanup of cellular debris from sites of infection. Neutrophils and macrophages are the main phagocytic cells of the body, but macrophages are much larger and longer-lived than neutrophils. Some macrophages are important as antigen-presenting cells, cells that phagocytose and degrade microbes and present portions of these organisms to T cells, thereby activating the specific acquired immune response.

The white blood cell count rises during many disease states, such as infections and intoxications. Specific types of cells are associated with different illnesses and reflect the special function of that cell type in body defense. A fall in white cell count, which is called leukopenia, occurs in states such as debilitation, anaphylaxis, and overwhelming infection. In general, newborns have a high white blood cell count that gradually falls to the adult level during childhood. An exception is the lymphocyte count, which is low at birth, reaches its highest levels in the first four years of life, and thereafter falls gradually to a stable adult level.

Granulocytes

Granulocytes are characterized by the large number and chemical makeup of the granules occurring within the cytoplasm. The granules, or secretory vesicles, harbour potent chemicals important in immune responses, and thus these cells are important mediators of the inflammatory response. Granulocytes are the most numerous of the white cells and are approximately 12–15 micrometres in diameter, making them larger than red blood cells. They also have a multilobed nucleus, and because of this they are often called polymorphonuclear cells. The three types of granulocytes, neutrophils, eosinophils, and basophils, are distinguished by the colour that the granules stain when treated with a compound dye. The differences in staining characteristics reflect differences in the chemical composition of the granules.

Granulocytes have a life span of only a few days and are continuously produced from stem cells (i.e., precursor cells) in the bone marrow. They enter the bloodstream and circulate for a few hours, after which they leave the circulation and die. Granulocytes are mobile and are attracted to foreign materials by chemical signals, some of which are produced by the invading microorganisms themselves, others by damaged tissues, and still others by the interaction between microbes and proteins in the blood plasma. Some microorganisms produce toxins that poison granulocytes and thus escape phagocytosis, whereas other microbes are indigestible and are not killed when ingested. As a result, granulocytes are of limited effectiveness by themselves and require reinforcement by the mechanisms of specific immunity (e.g., antibody-mediated immunity).

Neutrophils

Neutrophils are characterized histologically by their ability to be stained by neutral dyes and functionally by their role in mediating immune responses against infectious microorganisms. The granules of neutrophils typically stain pink or purple-blue following treatment with a dye. Neutrophils are the most numerous of the granulocytes and make up about 50 to 80 percent of all the white bloods cells occurring in the human body.

The neutrophils are fairly uniform in size with a diameter between 12 and 15 micrometres. The nucleus consists of two to five lobes joined together by hairlike filaments. Neutrophils move with amoeboid motion. They extend long projections called pseudopodia into which their granules flow, then they contract their filaments based in the cytoplasm, which draws the nucleus and rear of the cell forward. In this way neutrophils rapidly advance along a surface. The bone marrow of a normal adult produces about 100 billion neutrophils daily. It takes about one week to form a mature neutrophil from a precursor cell in the marrow. Yet, once in the blood, the mature cells live only a few hours or perhaps a little longer after migrating to the tissues. To guard against rapid depletion of the short-lived neutrophil (for example, during infection), the bone marrow holds a large number of them in reserve to be mobilized in response to inflammation or infection.

Within the body the neutrophils migrate to areas of infection or tissue injury. The force of attraction that determines the direction in which neutrophils will move is known as chemotaxis and is attributed to substances liberated at sites of tissue damage. Of the 100 billion neutrophils circulating outside the bone marrow, half are in the tissues and half are in the blood vessels. Of those in the blood vessels, half are within the mainstream of rapidly circulating blood and the other half move slowly along the inner walls of the blood vessels (marginal pool), ready to enter tissues on receiving a chemotactic signal from them.

Neutrophils are actively phagocytic. They engulf bacteria and other microorganisms and microscopic particles. The granules of the neutrophil are microscopic packets of potent enzymes capable of digesting many types of cellular materials. When a bacterium is engulfed by a neutrophil, it is encased in a vacuole lined by the invaginated membrane. The granules discharge their contents into the vacuole containing the organism. As this occurs, the granules of the neutrophil are depleted (degranulation). A metabolic process within the granules produces hydrogen peroxide and a highly active form of oxygen (superoxide), which destroy the ingested bacteria. Finally, enzymes digest the invading organism.

An abnormally high number of neutrophils circulating in the blood is called neutrophilia. This condition is typically associated with acute inflammation, but it may result from chronic myelogenous leukemia, a cancer of the blood-forming tissues. An abnormally low number of neutrophils is called neutropenia. This condition can be caused by various inherited disorders that affect the immune system as well as by a number of acquired diseases, including certain disorders that arise from exposure to harmful chemicals. Neutropenia significantly increases the risk of life-threatening bacterial infection.

Eosinophils

Eosinophils are characterized histologically by their ability to be stained by acidic dyes (e.g., eosin) and functionally by their role in mediating certain types of allergic reactions. Eosinophils contain large granules, and the nucleus exists as two nonsegmented lobes. In addition, the granules of eosinophils typically stain red, which makes them easily distinguished from other granulocytes when viewed on prepared slides under a microscope. Eosinophils are rare, making up less than 1 percent of the total number of white blood cells occurring in the human body.

Eosinophils, like other granulocytes, are produced in the bone marrow and then released into the circulation. Eosinophils leave the circulation within hours of release from the marrow and migrate into the tissues (usually those of the skin, lung, and respiratory tract) through the lymphatic channels. Similar to neutrophils, eosinophils respond to chemotactic signals released at the site of cell destruction. These chemical signals orient eosinophils and stimulate them to migrate in the direction of cell damage. Eosinophils are actively motile and phagocytic and participate in hypersensitivity and inflammatory reactions, primarily by dampening their destructive effects.

Eosinophils also are involved in defense against parasites. Eosinophils and antibodies of the immunoglobulin E (IgE) class work together to destroy parasites such as the flatworms that cause schistosomiasis. The eosinophils plaster themselves to the worms bound to IgE and release chemicals from their granules that break down the parasite's tough, protective skin.

Basophils

Basophils are characterized histologically by their ability to be stained by basic dyes and functionally by their role in mediating hypersensitivity reactions of the immune system. Basophils are the least numerous of the granulocytes and account for less than 1 percent of all white blood cells occurring in the human body.

Basophils contain large granules that stain purple-black in colour and almost completely obscure the underlying double-lobed nucleus. Within hours of their release from the bone marrow, basophils migrate from the circulation to the barrier tissues (e.g., the skin and mucosa), where they synthesize and store histamine, a natural modulator of the inflammatory response. When antibodies of the IgE class bind to specialized receptor molecules on basophils, the cells release their stores of inflammatory chemicals, including histamine, serotonin, and leukotrienes. These chemicals have a number of effects, including constriction of the smooth muscles, which leads to breathing difficulty; dilation of blood vessels, causing skin flush and hives; and an increase in vascular permeability, resulting in swelling and a decrease in blood pressure. Basophils also incite immediate hypersensitivity reactions in association with platelets, macrophages, and neutrophils.

Monocytes

Monocytes are the largest cells of the blood (averaging 15–18 micrometres). The nucleus is relatively big and tends to be indented or folded rather than multilobed. The cytoplasm contains large numbers of fine granules, which often appear to be more numerous near the cell membrane. Monocytes are actively motile and phagocytic. They are capable of ingesting infectious agents as well as red cells and other large particles, but they cannot replace the function of the neutrophils in the removal and destruction of bacteria. Monocytes usually enter areas of inflamed tissue later than the granulocytes. Often they are found at sites of chronic infections.

In the bone marrow, granulocytes and monocytes arise from a common precursor under the influence of the granulocyte-macrophage colony-stimulating factor. Monocytes leave the bone marrow and circulate in the blood. After a period of hours, the monocytes enter the tissues, where they develop into macrophages, the tissue phagocytes that constitute the reticuloendothelial system (or macrophage system). Macrophages occur in almost all tissues of the body: those in the liver are called Kupffer cells, those in the skin Langerhans cells. Apart from their role as scavengers, macrophages play a key role in immunity by ingesting antigens and processing them so that they can be recognized as foreign substances by lymphocytes.

Lymphocytes

Lymphocytes constitute about 28–42 percent of the white cells of the blood, and they are part of the immune response to foreign substances in the body. Most lymphocytes are small, only slightly larger than red blood cells, with a nucleus that occupies most of the cell. Some are larger and have more abundant cytoplasm that contains a few granules. Lymphocytes are sluggishly motile, and their paths of migration outside of the bloodstream are different from those of granulocytes and monocytes.

Lymphocytes are found in large numbers in the lymph nodes, spleen, thymus, tonsils, and lymphoid tissue of the gastrointestinal tract. They enter the circulation through lymphatic channels that drain principally into the thoracic lymph duct, which has a connection with the venous system. Unlike other blood cells, some lymphocytes may leave and reenter the circulation, surviving for about one year or more. The principal paths of recirculating lymphocytes are through the spleen or lymph nodes. Lymphocytes freely leave the blood to enter lymphoid tissue, passing barriers that prevent the passage of other blood cells. When stimulated by antigen and certain other agents, some lymphocytes are activated and become capable of cell division (mitosis).

The lymphocytes regulate or participate in the acquired immunity to foreign cells and antigens. They are responsible for immunologic reactions to invading organisms, foreign cells such as those of a transplanted organ, and foreign proteins and other antigens not necessarily derived from living cells. The two classes of lymphocytes are not distinguished by the usual microscopic examination but rather by the type of immune response they elicit. The B lymphocytes (or B cells) are involved in what is called humoral immunity. Upon encountering a foreign substance (or antigen), the B cell differentiates into a plasma cell, which secretes immuno-globulin (antibodies). The second class of lymphocytes, the T lymphocytes (or T cells), are involved in regulating the antibody-forming function of B cells as well as in directly attacking foreign antigens. T cells participate in what is called the cell-mediated immune response, in the rejection of transplanted tissues, and in certain types of allergic reactions.

All lymphocytes begin their development in the bone marrow. The B cells mature partly in the bone marrow until they are released into the circulation. Further differentiation of B cells occurs in lymphoid tissues (spleen or lymph nodes), most notably on stimulation by a foreign antigen. The precursors of the T cells migrate from the marrow to the thymus, where they differentiate under the influence of a hormonelike substance. (The thymus is a small organ lying just behind the breastbone in the upper portion of the chest. It is relatively large at birth, begins to regress after puberty, and may be represented only by a fibrous cord in the elderly. The thymus begins to exert its effects on the differentiation of lymphocytes before birth. The removal of the thymus from certain animals at birth prevents the normal development of immuno-logic responses.) Once they have matured, the T cells leave the thymus and circulate through the blood to the lymph nodes and the spleen. The two classes of lymphocytes originally derived their names from investigations in birds, in which it was found that differentiation of one class of lymphocyte was influenced by the bursa of Fabricius (an outpouching of the gastrointestinal tract) and thus was called the B cells, and the other was influenced by the thymus and called the T cells.

A primary function of lymphocytes is to protect the body from foreign microbes. This essential task is carried out by both T cells and B cells, which often act in concert. The T cells can only recognize and respond to antigens that appear on cell membranes in association with other molecules called major histocompatibility complex (MHC) antigens. The latter are glycoproteins that present the antigen in a form that can be recognized by T cells. In effect, T cells are responsible for continuous surveillance of cell surfaces for the presence of foreign antigens. By contrast, the antibodies produced by B cells are not confined to recognizing antigens on cell membranes. They can bind to soluble antigens in the blood or extravascular fluids. T cells typically recognize antigens of infectious organisms that must penetrate cells in order to multiply, such as viruses. During their intracellular life cycle, viruses produce antigens that appear on the cell membrane. Two classes of T cells can be involved in the response to those cell-associated viral antigens: cytotoxic T cells, which destroy the cells by a lytic mechanism, and helper T cells, which assist B cells to produce antibodies against the microbial antigens. Helper T cells exert their influence on B cells through several hormonelike peptides termed interleukins (IL). Five different T cell interleukins (IL-2, IL-3, IL-4, IL-5, and IL-6) have been discovered, each with different (and sometimes overlapping) effects on B cells and other blood cells. Interleukin-1, produced by macrophages, is a peptide that stimulates T cells and that also acts on the hypothalamus in the brain to produce fever. The ability to develop an immune response (i.e., the T cell-mediated and humoral immune responses) to foreign substances is called immunologic competence (immunocompetence). Immunologic competence, which begins to develop during embryonic life, is incomplete at the time of birth but is fully established soon after birth. If an antigen is introduced into the body before immunologic competence has been established, an immune response will not result upon reinfection, and that person is said to be tolerant to that antigen.

Study of immunologic competence and immune tolerance has been accelerated by interest in organ transplantation. The success rates of organ transplantations have been improved by better knowledge about donor selection and improved techniques for suppressing the immune responses of the recipient. An important element in donor selection is tissue typing: the matching of the donor's histocompatibility antigens (human leukocyte antigens) with those of the prospective recipient. The closer the match, the greater the probability that the graft will be accepted.

Platelets

The blood platelets are the smallest cells of the blood, averaging about 2-4 micrometres in diameter. Although much more numerous (150,000-400,000 per cubic millimetre) than the white cells, they occupy a much smaller fraction of the volume of the blood because of their relatively minute size. Like the red cells, they lack a nucleus and are incapable of cell division (mitosis), but they have a more complex metabolism and internal structure. When seen in fresh blood they appear spheroid, but they have a tendency to extrude hairlike filaments from their membranes. They adhere to each other but not to red cells and white cells. Tiny granules within platelets contain substances important for the clot-promoting activity of platelets.

The function of the platelets is related to hemostasis, the prevention and control of bleeding. When the endothelial surface (lining) of a blood vessel is injured, copious platelets immediately attach to the injured surface and to each other, forming a tenaciously adherent mass of platelets. The effect of the platelet response is to stop the bleeding and form the site of the developing blood clot, or thrombus. If platelets are absent, this important defense reaction cannot occur, resulting in protracted bleeding from small wounds (prolonged bleeding time). The normal resistance of capillary membranes to leakage of red cells depends on platelets. Severe deficiency of platelets reduces the resistance of the capillary walls, and abnormal bleeding from the capillaries occurs, either spontaneously or as the result of minor injury. Platelets also contribute substances essential for the normal coagulation of the blood, and they cause a clot to shrink or retract after it has been formed.

Platelets are formed in the bone marrow by segmentation of the cytoplasm (the cell substance other than the nucleus) of cells known as megakaryocytes, the largest cells of the marrow. Within the marrow the abundant granular cytoplasm of the megakaryocyte divides into many small segments that break off and are released as platelets into the circulating blood. After about 10 days in the circulation, platelets are removed and destroyed. There are no reserve stores of platelets except in the spleen, in which platelets occur in higher concentration than in the peripheral blood. Some platelets are consumed in exerting their hemostatic effects, and others, reaching the end of their life span, are removed by reticuloendothelial cells (any of the tissue phagocytes). The rate of platelet production is controlled but not so precisely as the control of red cell production. A hormonelike substance called thrombopoietin is believed to be the chemical mediator that regulates the number of platelets in the blood by stimulating an increase in the number and growth of megakaryocytes, thus controlling the rate of platelet production.

BLOOD CELL FORMATION

The continuous process by which the cellular constituents of blood are replenished as needed is known as blood cell formation, or hematopoiesis. Blood cells do not originate in the bloodstream itself but in specific blood-forming organs, notably the marrow of certain bones. In the human adult, the bone marrow produces all the red blood cells, 60–70 percent of the white cells (i.e., the granulocytes), and all the platelets. The lymphatic tissues, particularly the thymus, spleen, and lymph nodes, produce the lymphocytes (comprising 20–30 percent of the white cells). The reticuloendothelial tissues of the spleen, liver, lymph nodes, and other organs produce the monocytes (4–8 percent of the white cells). The platelets, which are small cellular fragments rather than complete cells, are formed

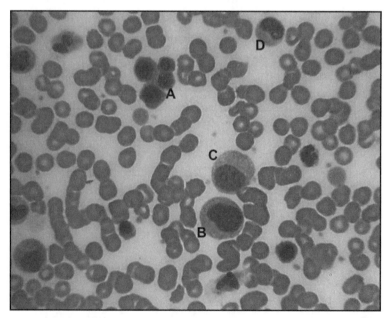

Bone marrow smear showing a cluster of erythroid cells (A), neutrophilic myelocytes (B and C), and an early neutrophilic metamyelocyte (D). Uniformed Services University of the Health Sciences (USUHS)

from bits of the cytoplasm of the giant cells (megakaryocytes) of the bone marrow.

In the human embryo, the first site of blood formation is the yolk sac. Later in embryonic life, the liver becomes the most important red blood cell–forming organ, but it is soon succeeded by the bone marrow, which in adult life is the only source of red blood cells as well as the granulocytes. Both the red and white blood cells arise through a series of complex, gradual, and successive transformations from primitive stem cells, which have the ability to form any of the precursors of a blood cell. Precursor cells are stem cells that have developed to the stage where they are committed to forming a particular kind of new blood cell.

In a normal adult, the red cells of about half a litre (almost one pint) of blood are produced by the bone marrow every week. Almost 1 percent of the body's red cells are generated each day, and the balance between red cell production and the removal of aging red cells from the circulation is precisely maintained. The rate of blood cell formation varies depending on the individual, but a typical production might average 200,000,000,000 red cells per day, 10,000,000,000 white cells per day, and 400,000,000,000 platelets per day.

BONE MARROW

The soft, gelatinous tissue that fills the cavities of the bones is known as bone marrow, or myeloid tissue. Bone marrow is either red or yellow, depending on the preponderance of hematopoietic (red) or fatty (yellow) tissue. In humans the red bone marrow forms all the blood cells with the exception of the lymphocytes, which are produced in the marrow and reach their mature form in the lymphoid organs. Red bone marrow also contributes, along with the liver and spleen, to the destruction of old red blood cells. Yellow bone marrow primarily serves as a storehouse for fats but may be converted to red marrow under certain conditions, such as severe blood loss or fever. At birth and until about the age of seven, all human marrow is red, because the need for new blood formation is high. Thereafter, fat tissue gradually replaces the red marrow, which in adults is found only in the vertebrae, hips, breastbone, ribs, and skull and at the ends of the long bones of the arm and leg. Other cancellous, or spongy, bones and the central cavities of the long bones are filled with yellow marrow.

Red marrow consists of a delicate, highly vascular fibrous tissue containing stem cells, which differentiate into various blood cells. Stem cells first become precursors, or blast cells, of various kinds. Erythroblasts give rise to the red blood cells, and myeloblasts become the granulocytes. Platelets form from megakaryocytes. The new blood cells are released into the sinusoids, large thin-walled vessels that drain into the veins of the bone. In mammals, blood formation in adults predominantly takes place in the marrow. In lower vertebrates a number of other tissues may also produce blood cells, including the liver and the spleen.

Because the white blood cells produced in the bone marrow are involved in the body's immune defenses, marrow transplants have been used to treat certain types of immune deficiency and hematological disorders, especially leukemia. The sensitivity of marrow to damage by radiation therapy and some anticancer drugs accounts for the tendency of these treatments to impair immunity and blood production.

Examination of the bone marrow helps diagnose certain diseases, especially those related to blood and blood-forming organs, because it provides information on iron stores and blood production. Bone marrow aspiration, the direct removal of a small amount (about 1 ml) of bone marrow, is accomplished by suction through a hollow needle. The needle is usually inserted into the hip or sternum (breastbone) in adults and into the upper part of the tibia (the larger bone of the lower leg) in children. The necessity for a bone marrow aspiration is ordinarily based on previous blood studies and is particularly useful in providing information on various stages of immature blood cells. Disorders in which bone marrow examination is of special diagnostic value include leukemia, multiple myeloma, Gaucher disease, unusual cases of anemia, and other hematological diseases.

PRODUCTION OF RED BLOOD CELLS

Red blood cell production, or erythropoiesis, is a continuous process. In adults the principal sites of red cell production are the marrow spaces of the vertebrae, ribs, breastbone, and pelvis. Within the bone marrow the red cell is derived from a primitive precursor, or erythroblast, a nucleated cell in which there is no hemoglobin. Proliferation occurs as a result of several successive cell divisions. During maturation, hemoglobin appears in the cell, and the nucleus becomes progressively smaller. After a few days the cell loses its nucleus and is then introduced into the bloodstream in the vascular channels of the marrow. When blood is lost from the circulation, the erythropoietic activity of marrow increases until the normal number of circulating cells has been restored.

A number of nutrient substances are required for red cell production. Some nutrients are the building blocks of which the red cells are composed. For example, amino acids are needed in abundance for the construction of the proteins of the red cell, in particular of hemoglobin. Iron also is a necessary component of hemoglobin. Approximately one-quarter of a gram of iron is needed for the production of a pint of blood. Other substances, required in trace amounts, are needed to catalyze the chemical reactions by which red cells are produced. Important among these are several vitamins such as riboflavin, vitamin B_{12}, and folic acid, necessary for the maturation of the developing red cell; and vitamin B_6 (pyridoxine), required for the synthesis of hemoglobin. The secretions of several endocrine glands influence red cell production. If there is an inadequate supply of thyroid hormone, erythropoiesis is retarded and anemia appears. The male sex hormone, testosterone, stimulates red cell production. Thus, red cell counts of men are higher than those of women.

The capacity of the bone marrow to produce red cells is enormous. When stimulated to peak activity and when provided adequately with nutrient substances, the marrow can compensate for the loss of several pints of blood per week. Hemorrhage or accelerated destruction of red cells leads to enhanced marrow activity. The marrow can increase its production of red cells up to eight times the usual rate. After that, if blood loss continues, anemia develops. The rate of erythropoiesis is sensitive to the oxygen tension of the arterial blood. When oxygen tension falls, more red cells are produced and the red cell count rises. For this reason, persons who live at high altitude have higher red cell counts than those who live at sea level. For example, there is a small but significant difference between average red cell counts of persons living in New York City, at sea level pressure, and persons living in Denver, Colo., more than 1.5 km (1 mile) above sea level, where the atmospheric pressure is lower. Natives of the Andes, living nearly 5 km (3 miles) above sea level, have extremely high red cell counts.

The rate of production of red blood cells is controlled by the hormone erythropoietin, which is produced largely in the kidneys. When the number of circulating red cells decreases or when the oxygen transported by the blood diminishes, an unidentified sensor detects the change and the production of erythropoietin is increased. This substance is then transported through the plasma to the bone marrow, where it accelerates the production of red cells. The erythropoietin mechanism operates like a thermostat, increasing or decreasing the rate of red cell production in accordance with need. When a person who has lived at high altitude moves to a sea level environment, production of erythropoietin is suppressed, the rate of red cell production declines, and the red cell count falls until the normal sea level value is achieved. With the loss of one pint of blood, the erythropoietin mechanism is activated, red cell production is enhanced, and within a few weeks the number of circulating red cells has been restored to the normal value. The precision of control is extraordinary so that the number of new red cells produced accurately compensates for the number of cells lost or destroyed. Erythropoietin has been produced in vitro (outside the body) by the technique of genetic engineering (recombinant DNA). The purified, recombinant hormone has promise for persons with chronic renal failure, who develop anemia because of a lack of erythropoietin.

DESTRUCTION OF RED BLOOD CELLS

Survival of the red blood cell in the circulation depends on the continuous use of glucose for the production of energy. Two chemical pathways are employed, and both are essential for the normal life of the red cell. An extraordinary number of enzyme systems participate in these reactions and direct the energy evolved into appropriate uses. Red cells contain neither a nucleus nor RNA (ribonucleic acid, necessary for protein synthesis), so cell division and production of new protein are impossible. Energy is unnecessary for oxygen and carbon dioxide transport, which depends principally on the properties of hemoglobin. Energy, however, is needed for another reason. Because extracellular sodium tends to leak into the red cell and potassium tends to leak out, energy is required to operate a pumping mechanism in the red cell membrane to maintain the normal gradients (differences in concentrations) of these ions. Energy is also required to convert methemoglobin to oxyhemoglobin and to prevent the oxidation of other constituents of the red cell.

Because red cells cannot synthesize protein, reparative processes are impossible. As red cells age, wear and tear leads to loss of some of their protein, and the activity of some of their essential enzymes decreases. Chemical reactions necessary for the survival of the cell are consequently impaired. As a result, water passes into the aging red cell, transforming its usual discoid shape into a sphere. As these inelastic spherocytes sluggishly move through the circulation, they are engulfed by phagocytes. Phagocytic cells form a part of the lining of blood vessels, particularly in the spleen, liver, and bone marrow. These cells, called macrophages, are constituents of the reticuloendothelial system and are found in the lymph nodes, in the intestinal tract, and as free-wandering and fixed cells. As a group they have the ability to ingest not only other cells but also many other microscopic particles, including certain dyes and colloids. Within the reticuloendothelial cells, red cells are rapidly destroyed. Protein, including that of the hemoglobin, is broken down, and the component amino acids are transported through the plasma to be used in the synthesis of new proteins. The iron removed from hemo-globin passes back into the plasma and is transported to the bone marrow, where it may be used in the synthesis of hemoglobin in newly forming red cells. Iron that is not for this purpose is stored within the reticuloendothelial cells but is available for release and reuse whenever it is required. In the breakdown of red cells, there is no loss to the body of either protein or iron, virtually all of which is conserved and reused. In contrast, the porphyrin ring structure of hemoglobin, to which iron was attached, undergoes a chemical change that enables its excretion from the body. This reaction converts porphyrin, a red pigment, into bilirubin, a yellow pigment. Bilirubin released from reticuloendothelial cells after the destruc-tion of red cells is conveyed through the plasma to the liver, where it undergoes further changes that prepare it for secretion into the bile. The amount of bilirubin pro-duced and secreted into the bile is determined by the amount of hemoglobin destroyed. When the rate of red cell destruction exceeds the capacity of the liver to handle bilirubin, the yellow pigment accumulates in the blood, causing jaundice. Jaundice can also occur if the liver is dis-eased (e.g., hepatitis) or if the egress of bile is blocked (e.g., by a gallstone).

CHAPTER 2

THE DYNAMICS OF BLOOD

Blood conveys vital nutrients to cells throughout the body. In order to reach these microscopic entities, it must travel through a series of blood vessels. These vessels, along with the heart and lungs, make up the primary elements of the circulatory system. This system facilitates the continuous movement of blood, enabling the efficient delivery of oxygen and other nutrients to the tissues of the body, as well as the swift removal of carbon dioxide and other wastes.

Components of the circulatory system, including blood pressure and hemostasis (the prevention and control of bleeding), play important roles in maintaining the proper function of circulatory processes. The dynamic nature of blood is illustrated by high-pressure blood circulation, in which a single breach in a vessel wall can cause severe bleeding. When a blood vessel is damaged, cells surrounding it send out emergency signals that activate a protein capable of initiating the process of clotting. For this process to be effective, cells must respond quickly, and thus the coagulation (clot formation) system consists of a rapid cascade of reactions that culminates in the arrest of bleeding. Such active responses of blood form a vital part of its life-sustaining ability and demonstrate that, in addition to nutrient delivery to and waste removal from tissues, it has important functions in maintaining normal circulatory mechanisms.

CIRCULATION

Circulation is the process by which nutrients, respiratory gases, and metabolic products are transported throughout

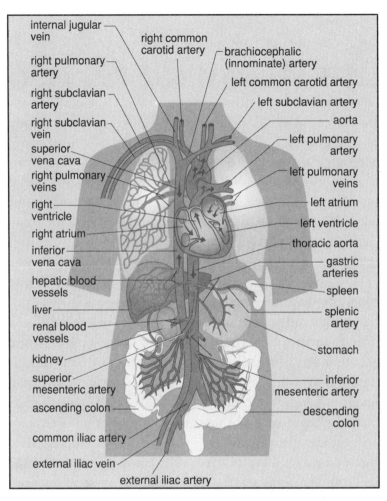

Human circulatory system. The pulmonary circulation consists of the right ventricle and the exiting pulmonary artery and its branches (the arterioles, capillaries, and venules of the lung) and the pulmonary vein. Unlike the other arteries and veins, the pulmonary arteries carry deoxygenated blood and the pulmonary veins carry oxygenated blood. The aorta arises from the left ventricle. The brachiocephalic artery arises from the aorta and divides into the right common carotid and right subclavian arteries. The left and right common carotids extend on either side of the neck and supply much of the head and neck. The left subclavian artery (arising from the aorta) and the right subclavian artery supply the arms. In the lower abdomen, the aorta divides into the common iliac arteries, which give rise to external and internal branches supplying the legs. © Merriam-Webster Inc.

the body. In humans, blood remains within a closed cardiovascular system composed of the heart, blood vessels, and blood. Arteries carry blood away from the heart under high pressure exerted by the heart's pumping action. Arteries divide into smaller arterioles, which branch into a network of tiny capillaries with thin walls across which gases and nutrients diffuse. Capillaries rejoin into larger venules, which unite to form veins, which in turn carry blood back to the heart. The right and left heart chambers send blood into separate pulmonary and systemic circulations. In the first, blood is carried from the heart to the lungs, where it picks up oxygen and releases carbon dioxide. In the second, blood is carried between the heart and the rest of the body, where it carries oxygen, nutrients, metabolic products, and wastes.

ARTERIES

Arteries are any of the vessels that, with one exception, carry oxygenated blood and nourishment from the heart to the tissues of the body. The exception, the pulmonary artery, carries oxygen-depleted blood to the lungs for oxygenation and removal of excess carbon dioxide.

Arteries are muscular and elastic tubes that must transport blood under a high pressure exerted by the pumping action of the heart. The pulse, which can be felt over an artery lying near the surface of the skin, results from the alternate expansion and contraction of the arterial wall as the beating heart forces blood into the arterial system via the aorta. Large arteries branch off from the aorta and in turn give rise to smaller arteries until the level of the smallest arteries, or arterioles, is reached. The threadlike arterioles carry blood to networks of microscopic vessels called capillaries, which

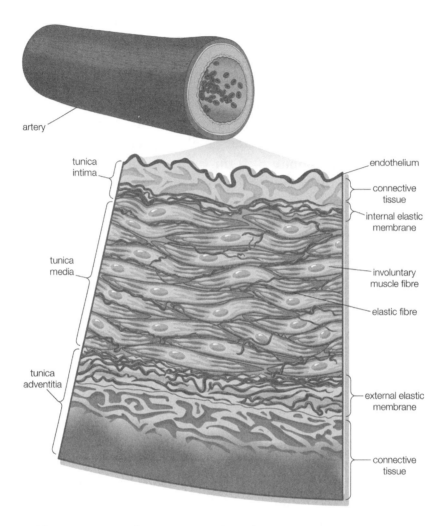

Transverse section of an artery. Encyclopædia Britannica, Inc.

supply nourishment and oxygen to the tissues and carry away carbon dioxide and other products of metabolism by way of the veins.

The largest artery is the aorta, which arises from the left ventricle of the heart. The aorta arches briefly upward before continuing downward close to the backbone; the arteries that supply blood to the head, neck, and arms arise from this arch and travel upward. As it descends along the backbone, the aorta gives rise to other major arteries that supply the internal organs of the thorax. After descending to the abdomen, the aorta divides into two terminal branches, each of which supplies blood to one leg.

Each artery, no matter what its size, has walls with three layers, or coats. The innermost layer, or tunica intima, consists of a lining, a fine network of connective tissue, and a layer of elastic fibres bound together in a membrane pierced with many openings. Principally, the tunica media, or middle coat, is made up of smooth (involuntary) muscle cells and elastic fibres arranged in roughly spiral layers. The outermost coat, or tunica adventitia, is a tough layer consisting mainly of collagen fibres that act as a supportive element. The large arteries differ structurally from the medium-sized arteries in that they have a much thicker tunica media and a some-what thicker tunica adventitia.

VEINS

Veins are any of the vessels that, with four exceptions, carry oxygen-depleted blood to the right upper chamber (atrium) of the heart. The four exceptions—the pulmonary veins— transport oxygenated blood from the lungs to the left upper chamber of the heart. The oxygen-depleted blood transported by most veins is collected from the networks of microscopic vessels called capillaries by thread-sized veins called venules.

As in the arteries, the walls of veins have three layers, or coats: an inner layer, or tunica intima; a middle layer, or tunica media; and an outer layer, or tunica adventitia. Each coat has a number of sublayers. The tunica intima differs from the inner layer of an artery. Many veins, particularly in the arms and legs, have valves to prevent backflow of blood, and the elastic membrane lining the artery is absent in the vein, which consists primarily of endothelium and scant connective tissue. The tunica media, which in an artery is composed of muscle and elastic fibres, is thinner in a vein and contains less muscle and elastic tissue, and proportionately more collagen fibres (collagen, a fibrous protein, is the main supporting element in connective tissue). The outer layer (tunica adventitia) consists chiefly of connective tissue and is the thickest layer of the vein. As in arteries, there are tiny vessels called vasa vasorum that supply blood to the walls of the veins and other minute vessels that carry blood away. Veins are more numerous than arteries and have thinner walls owing to lower blood pressure. They tend to parallel the course of arteries.

Capillaries

Capillaries are any of the minute blood vessels that form networks throughout the bodily tissues. Oxygen, nutrients, and wastes are exchanged between the blood and the tissues through the capillaries. The capillary networks are the ultimate destination of arterial blood from the heart and are the starting point for flow of venous blood back to the heart. Between the smallest arteries, or arterioles, and the capillaries are intermediate vessels called precapillaries, or metarterioles, that, unlike the capillaries, have muscle fibres that permit them to contract. Thus the precapillaries can control the emptying and filling of the capillaries.

The capillaries are about 8–10 micrometres (a micrometre is 0.001 mm) in diameter, just large enough for red blood cells to pass through them in single file. The single layer of cells that form their walls are endothelial cells, like those that form the smooth channel surface of the larger vessels.

The networks of capillaries have meshes of varying size. In the lungs and choroid—the middle coat of the eyeball—the spaces between capillaries are smaller than the vessels themselves, whereas in the outer coat of arteries—the tunica adventitia—the intercapillary spaces are about 10 times greater than the diameter of the capillaries. In general, the intercapillary spaces are smaller in growing parts, the glands, and the mucous membranes; larger in bones and ligaments; and almost absent in tendons.

The smallest vessels in the lymphatic system are also called capillaries, as are the minute channels for bile in the liver.

BLOOD PRESSURE

Blood pressure is the force exerted by the blood against the walls of the blood vessels. This force originates with the pumping action of the heart, and the stretching of the vessels in response to this force and their subsequent contraction are important in maintaining blood flow through the vascular system.

Blood pressure is usually measured indirectly over the brachial artery (in the arm) or femoral artery (in the leg). There are two pressures measured: (1) the systolic pressure (the higher pressure and the first number recorded), which is the force that blood exerts on the artery walls as the heart contracts to pump the blood to the peripheral organs and tissues, and (2) the diastolic pressure (the lower pressure and the second number recorded), which is residual pressure exerted on the arteries as the heart relaxes between beats. In healthy individuals, systolic pressure is normally between 100 and 140 millimetres of mercury (mmHg). Diastolic pressure is normally between 60 and 100 mmHg. Studies have shown that there are stark contrasts in the blood pressure of vessels of different sizes; for example, blood pressure in the capillaries is usually about 20 to 30 mmHg, whereas the pressure in the large veins may become negative (lower than atmospheric pressure [760 mmHg at sea level]; technically, measurements of blood pressure are relative to atmospheric pressure, which represents the "zero reference point" for blood pressure readings).

Arterial blood pressure varies among individuals and in the same individual from time to time. It is lower in children than in adults and increases gradually with age. It tends to be higher in those who are overweight. During sleep it decreases slightly, and during exercise and emotional excitement it increases.

FUNCTIONS OF BLOOD

Broadly conceived, the function of the blood is to maintain the constancy of the internal environment. The circulating blood makes possible adaptability to changing conditions of life: the endurance of wide variations of climate and atmospheric pressure; the capacity to alter the amount of physical activity; the tolerance of changing diet and fluid intake; and the resistance to physical injury, chemical poisons, and infectious agents. The blood has an exceedingly complex structure, and many components participate in its functional activities. Some regulatory mechanisms with which the blood is involved include sensors that detect alterations in temperature, pH, oxygen tension, and concentrations of the constituents of the blood. Effects of these stimuli are in some instances mediated via the nervous system or by the release of hormones (chemical mediators).

RESPIRATION

In terms of immediate urgency, the respiratory function of the blood is vital. A continuous supply of oxygen is required by living cells, in particular those of the brain, since deprivation results in unconsciousness and death within minutes. A normal male at rest uses about 250 ml of oxygen per minute, a requirement increased manyfold during vigorous exertion. All this oxygen is transported by the blood, most of it bound to the hemoglobin of the red cells. The minute blood vessels of the lungs bring the blood into close apposition with the pulmonary air spaces (alveoli), where the pressure of oxygen is relatively high. Oxygen diffuses through the plasma and into the red cell, combining with hemoglobin, which is about 95 percent saturated with oxygen on leaving the lungs. One gram of hemoglobin can bind 1.35 ml of oxygen, and about 50 times as much oxygen is combined with hemoglobin as is dissolved in the plasma. In tissues where the oxygen tension is relatively low, hemoglobin releases the bound oxygen.

The two main regulators of oxygen uptake and delivery are the pH (a measure of the acidity or basicity) of tissues and the content in red cells of an anionic (negatively charged) organic phosphate compound known as 2,3-diphosphoglycerate (2,3-DPG). The pH of blood is kept relatively constant at the slightly alkaline level of about 7.4 (pH less than 7 indicates acidity, more than 7 alkalinity). The effect of pH on the ability of hemoglobin to bind oxygen is called the Bohr effect: when pH is low, hemoglobin binds oxygen less strongly, and when pH is high (as in the lungs), hemoglobin binds more tightly to oxygen. The Bohr effect is caused by changes in the shape of the hemoglobin molecule as the pH of its environment changes. The oxygen affinity of hemoglobin is also regulated by 2,3-DPG, a simple molecule produced by the red cell when it metabolizes glucose. The effect of 2,3-DPG is to reduce the oxygen affinity of hemoglobin. When the availability of oxygen to tissues is reduced, the red cell responds by synthesizing more 2,3-DPG, a process that occurs over a period of hours to days. By contrast, tissue pH mediates minute-to-minute changes in oxygen handling.

Carbon dioxide, a waste product of cellular metabolism, is found in relatively high concentration in the tissues. It diffuses into the blood and is carried to the lungs to be eliminated with the expired air. Carbon dioxide is much more soluble than oxygen and readily diffuses into red cells. It reacts with water to form carbonic acid, a weak acid that, at the alkaline pH of the blood, appears principally as bicarbonate.

The tension of carbon dioxide in the arterial blood is regulated with extraordinary precision through a sensing mechanism in the brain that controls the respiratory movements. Carbon dioxide is an acidic substance, and an increase in its concentration tends to lower the pH of the blood (i.e., becoming more acidic). This may be averted by the stimulus that causes increased depth and rate of breathing, a response that accelerates the loss of carbon dioxide. It is the tension of carbon dioxide, and not of oxygen, in the arterial blood that normally controls breathing. Inability to hold one's breath for more than a minute or so is the result of the rising tension of carbon dioxide, which produces the irresistible stimulus to breathe. Respiratory movements that ventilate the lungs sufficiently to maintain a normal tension of carbon dioxide are, under normal conditions, adequate to keep the blood fully oxygenated. Control of respiration is effective, therefore, in regulating the uptake of oxygen and disposal of carbon dioxide and in maintaining the constancy of blood pH.

Nutrition

Each substance required for the nutrition of every cell in the body is transported by the blood: the precursors of carbohydrates, proteins, and fats; minerals and salts; and vitamins and other accessory food factors. These substances must all pass through the plasma on the way to the tissues in which they are used. The materials may enter the bloodstream from the gastrointestinal tract, or they may be released from stores within the body or become available from the breakdown of tissue.

The concentrations of many plasma constituents, including blood sugar (glucose) and calcium, are carefully regulated, and deviations from the normal may have adverse effects. One glucose regulator is insulin, a hormone released into the blood from glandular cells in the pancreas. Ingestion of carbohydrates is followed by increased production of insulin, which tends to keep the blood glucose level from rising excessively as the carbohydrates are broken down into their constituent sugar molecules. But an excess of insulin may severely reduce the level of glucose in the blood, causing a reaction that, if sufficiently severe, may result in coma and even death.

Glucose is transported in simple solution, but some substances require specific binding proteins (with which the substances form temporary unions) to convey them through the plasma. Iron and copper, essential minerals, have special and necessary transport proteins. Nutrient substances may be taken up selectively by the tissues that require them. Growing bones use large amounts of calcium, and bone marrow removes iron from plasma for hemoglobin synthesis.

EXCRETION

The blood carries the waste products of cellular metabolism to the excretory organs. Water produced by the oxidation of foods or available from other sources in excess of needs is excreted by the kidneys as the solvent of the urine, and water derived from the blood also is lost from the body by evaporation from the skin and lungs as well as in small amounts from the gastrointestinal tract. The water content of the blood and of the body as a whole remains within a narrow range because of effective regulatory mechanisms, hormonal and other, that determine the urinary volume. The concentrations of physiologically important ions of the plasma, notably sodium, potassium, and chloride, are precisely controlled by their retention or selective removal as blood flows through the kidneys.

Of special significance is the renal (kidney) control of acidity of the urine, a major factor in the maintenance of the normal pH of the blood. Urea, creatinine, and uric acid are nitrogen-containing products of metabolism that are transported by the blood and rapidly eliminated by the kidneys. The kidneys clear the blood of many other substances, including numerous drugs and chemicals that are taken into the body. In performing their excretory function, the kidneys have a major responsibility for maintaining the constancy of the composition of the blood. The liver also is, in part, an excretory organ. Bilirubin (bile pigment) produced by the destruction of hemoglobin is conveyed by the plasma to the liver and is excreted through the biliary ducts into the gastrointestinal tract. Other substances, including certain drugs, also are removed from the plasma by the liver.

Hemostasis

The blood is contained under pressure in a vascular system that includes vast areas of thin and delicate capillary membranes. Even the bumps and knocks of everyday life are sufficient to disrupt some of these fragile vessels, and serious injury can be much more damaging. Blood loss would be a constant threat to survival if it were not for protective mechanisms to prevent and control bleeding. The platelets contribute to the resistance of capillaries, possibly because they actually fill chinks in vessel walls. In the absence of platelets, capillaries become more fragile, permitting spontaneous loss of blood and increasing the tendency to form bruises after minor injury. Platelets immediately aggregate at the site of injury of a blood vessel, tending to seal the aperture. A blood clot, forming

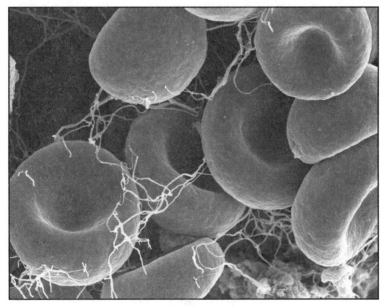

A scanning electron micrograph (SEM) showing the formation of a blot clot. Clots form as part of hemostasis, the body's ability to stem blood loss after vessel damage has occurred. Steve Gschmeissner/SPL/Getty Images

in the vessel around the clump of adherent platelets, further occludes the bleeding point. The coagulation mechanism involves a series of chemical reactions in which specific proteins and other constituents of the blood, including the platelets, play a part. Plasma also is provided with a mechanism for dissolving clots after they have been formed. Plasmin is a proteolytic enzyme — a substance that causes breakdown of proteins — derived from an inert plasma precursor known as plasminogen. When clots are formed within blood vessels, activation of plasminogen to plasmin may lead to their removal.

Immunity

Cells of the blood and constituents of the plasma interact in complex ways to confer immunity to infectious agents, resist or destroy invading organisms, produce the inflammatory response, and destroy and remove foreign materials and dead cells. The white blood cells have a primary role in these reactions. Granulocytes and monocytes phagocytize (ingest) bacteria and other organisms, migrate to sites of infection or inflammation and to areas containing dead tissue, and participate in the enzymatic breakdown and removal of cellular debris. Lymphocytes are concerned with the development of immunity.

Acquired resistance to specific microorganisms is in part attributable to antibodies, proteins formed in response to the entry into the body of a foreign substance (antigen). Antibodies that have been induced by microorganisms not only participate in eliminating the microbes but also prevent reinfection by the same organism. Cells and antibodies may cooperate in the destruction of invading bacteria. The antibody may attach to the organism, thereby rendering it susceptible to phagocytosis. Involved in some reactions is the complement, a group of protein components of plasma that participates in certain immunologic reactions. When certain classes of antibodies bind to microorganisms and other cells, they trigger the attachment of components of the complement system to the outer membrane of the target cell. As they assemble on the cell membrane, the complement components acquire enzymatic properties, and the activated complement system is thus able to injure the cell by digesting (lysing) portions of the cell's protective membrane.

Temperature Regulation

Heat is produced in large amounts by physiological oxidative reactions, and the blood is essential for its distributing and disposing of this heat. The circulation assures relative uniformity of temperature throughout the body and also carries the warm blood to the surface, where heat is lost to the external environment. A heat-regulating centre in the hypothalamus of the brain functions much like a thermostat. Sensitive to changes in temperature of the blood flowing through, it responds by giving off nerve impulses that control the diameter of the blood vessels in the skin and thus determines blood flow and skin temperature. A rise in skin temperature increases heat loss from the body surface. Heat is continuously lost by evaporation of water from the lungs and skin, but this loss can be greatly increased when more water is made available from the sweat glands. The activity of the sweat glands is controlled by the nervous system under direction of the temperature-regulating centre. Constancy of body temperature is achieved by control of the rate of heat loss by these mechanisms.

BLEEDING AND BLOOD CLOTTING

Bleeding is the escape of blood from vessels into surrounding tissue, and blood clotting, or coagulation, is the process by which a clot is formed to stop bleeding (hemostasis). The formation of a clot is often referred to as secondary hemostasis, because it forms the second stage in the process of arresting the loss of blood from a ruptured vessel. The first stage, primary hemostasis, is characterized by blood vessel constriction (vasoconstriction) and platelet aggregation at the site of vessel injury. Under abnormal circumstances, clots can also form in a vessel that has not been breached. Such clots can result in the occlusion (blockage) of the vessel.

SIGNIFICANCE OF HEMOSTASIS

The evolution of high-pressure blood circulation in vertebrates has brought with it the risk of bleeding after injury to tissues. Mechanisms to prevent bleeding (i.e., hemostatic mechanisms) are essential to maintain the closed blood-circulatory system. Normal hemostasis is the responsibility of a complex system of three individual components: (1) blood cells (platelets), (2) cells that line the blood vessels (endothelial cells), and (3) blood proteins (blood-clotting proteins). The blood platelet is a nonnucleated cell that circulates in the blood in an inactive, resting form. Endothelial cells line the wall of the blood vessel and inhibit blood from clotting on the vessel wall under normal conditions. Blood-clotting proteins circulate in the blood plasma in an inactive form, poised to participate in blood coagulation upon tissue injury. Blood-clotting proteins generate thrombin, an enzyme that converts fibrinogen to fibrin, and a reaction that leads to the formation of a fibrin clot.

The hemostatic mechanism involves three physiologically important reactions: (1) the formation of a blood clot, (2) the formation of a platelet plug, and (3) changes associated with the wall of the blood vessel after injury of its cells. In humans, defects in any of these processes may result in persistent bleeding from slight injuries, or, alternatively, an overreaction that causes the inappropriate formation of blood clots (thrombosis) in blood vessels. When a blood vessel is injured, blood escapes for as long as the vessel remains open and the pressure within the vessel exceeds that outside. Blood flow can be stopped or diminished by closing the leak or equalizing the pressure. The leak may be closed by contraction of the blood vessel wall or by the formation of a solid plug. Pressure may be equalized by an increase in external pressure as blood becomes trapped in the tissues (hematoma) or by decrease in the intravascular pressure (the pressure within the blood vessel) caused by constriction of a supply vessel. The timing and relative importance of these events can vary with the scale of the injury. Bleeding from the smallest vessels can be stopped by platelet plugs. When bleeding is from larger vessels, blood clot formation is required. Finally, in still larger vessels, the severe drop in pressure associated with shock is the last line of defense.

Prothrombin and Thrombin

Prothrombin is a glycoprotein (carbohydrate-protein compound) occurring in blood plasma and an essential component of the blood-clotting mechanism. Prothrombin is transformed into thrombin by a clotting factor known as factor X or prothrombinase. Thrombin then acts to transform fibrinogen, also present in plasma, into fibrin, which, in combination with platelets from the blood, forms a clot (the process of coagulation). Under normal circumstances, prothrombin is changed into thrombin only when injury occurs to the tissues or circulatory system or both. Therefore, fibrin and blood clots are only formed in response to bleeding.

Hypoprothrombinemia, a deficiency in prothrombin, is characterized by a tendency toward prolonged bleeding. It is usually associated with a lack of vitamin K, which is necessary for the synthesis of prothrombin in the liver cells. In adults the condition occurs most commonly in cases of obstructive jaundice, in which the flow of bile to the bowel is interrupted—bile being necessary for the intestinal absorption of vitamin K. It can also result from a general impairment in liver and intestinal-cell function or overdose of warfarin and related therapeutic anticoagulants.

Fibrin

Fibrin is an insoluble protein that is produced in response to bleeding and is the major component of the blood clot. Fibrin is a tough protein substance that is arranged in long

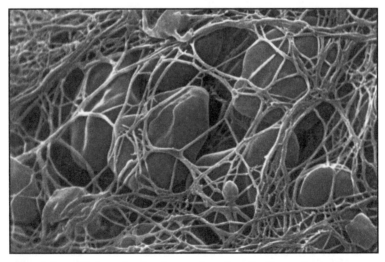

After injury, fibrin molecules elongate into threads that gather and act as a net, trapping and distorting red blood cells until they converge to form a clot. Dr. David Phillips/Visuals Unlimited/Getty Images

fibrous chains and formed from fibrinogen, a soluble protein that is produced by the liver and found in blood plasma. When tissue damage results in bleeding, fibrinogen is converted at the wound into fibrin by the action of thrombin. Fibrin molecules then combine to form long fibrin threads that entangle platelets, building up a spongy mass that gradually hardens and contracts to form the blood clot. This hardening process is stabilized by a substance known as fibrin-stabilizing factor, or factor XIII.

Certain rare hereditary disorders may cause malfunction of this stage of the blood-clotting mechanism. A few individuals have a hereditary deficiency of fibrinogen or produce abnormal fibrinogen. Upon injury to these persons, fibrin cannot form in sufficient quantity to enable a proper clot to form. Another rare hereditary disease involves a lack of factor XIII, resulting in a condition in which bleeding is difficult to stop.

THE HEMOSTATIC PROCESS

Blood vessels that constitute the circulatory system include arterioles (the smallest arteries) and venules (the smallest veins) connected by capillaries (the smallest of all blood vessels). Blood cells, including red cells and platelets, normally have no tendency to adhere to each other or to the lining (endothelium) of the vessels. An injury too slight to rupture a vessel, however, may still bring about a hemostatic reaction that causes blood cells to adhere to each other. After minor tissue injury, there may be partial vessel contraction and platelet adhesion in successive layers at the point of injury, which forms a platelet mass that grows until it blocks, or almost blocks, the vessel. Sometimes this platelet mass breaks down and then reforms, a cycle that may repeat many times. These masses consist of minimally altered platelets. Even these slight injuries cause shedding of some endothelial cells from the vessel and the exposure of deeper layers to which the platelets adhere.

If the vessel is cut so that blood escapes, the hemostatic reaction is different. In muscular vessels there may be immediate contraction and narrowing of the vessel, but this usually only minimizes blood loss. A mass of activated platelets adheres to the site of vessel injury (a platelet plug) and normally stops the flow of blood out of the vessel. Unlike the platelets circulating in the blood and those adhering to minor tissue injuries, these platelets have undergone a biochemical and morphological change characteristic of platelet activation, a process that includes the secretion of the contents of platelet granules into the surrounding blood and the extension of pseudopodia. Bundles of fibrin fibres develop between the platelets (coagulation). These changes occur near damaged collagen, the fibrous protein found in connective tissue that underlies the endothelial cell. Later, normal healing of the wound occurs. The platelets subsequently degenerate into an amorphous mass, and after several days, the fibrin itself is dissolved (fibrinolysis) by an enzyme known as plasmin. The fibrin clot is replaced by a permanent framework of scar tissue that includes collagen, and healing is thus complete.

The normal hemostatic response to damage to the vascular endothelium can be organized into four stages: (1) initial vasoconstriction, (2) aggregation of platelets on and around the lesion and the formation of a platelet plug, (3) activation of the reactions of coagulation, and (4) the activation of fibrinolysis.

Vascular Function

The most obvious hemostatic vascular reaction is constriction of the blood vessel after injury. This is important in large arteries because platelet adhesion and clotting are insufficient to arrest bleeding. Delayed surgical aid notwithstanding, the survival of some persons who have lost limbs in accidents is caused by constriction of their main arteries. Other vascular reactions to injury have only a subsidiary hemostatic effect.

Platelets and Their Aggregation

Mammalian platelets are nonnucleate cells produced by large bone marrow cells called megakaryocytes and circulate in the blood in a resting, inactive form for an average of 10 days. The normal platelet count in humans is between 150,000 and 400,000 platelets per cubic millimetre of blood. The inactive platelet contains three types of internal granules: alpha granules, dense granules, and lysosomes. Each of these granules is rich in certain chemicals that have an important role in platelet function. For example, dense granules contain large quantities of calcium ions and adenosine diphosphate (ADP). Upon release from the platelet, ADP stimulates other platelets to activate when it binds to the ADP receptor on the platelet membrane. The alpha granules contain many proteins, including fibrinogen, thrombospondin, fibronectin, and von Willebrand factor. Upon platelet activation, platelets alter their shape from discoid to spherical and extend long footlike projections called pseudopodia. The alpha granules and dense granules move to the surface of the platelet, fuse with the platelet membrane, and release their contents into the blood surrounding the platelet. The lysosomes contain enzymes that digest spent proteins and other metabolites of the cell.

Activated platelets strongly adhere to surfaces other than the lining of blood vessels, such as collagen, glass, metals, and fabrics. Adherent platelets themselves become adhesive for other activated platelets so that, in a flow system, a platelet plug develops. The propagation of this adhesiveness from one layer to the next is probably due to chemicals, such as ADP and thromboxane A_2, that are secreted into the blood from the granules of the activated platelets. The ADP released from the dense granules binds to a receptor on the platelet surface, initiating the biochemical and morphological changes associated with platelet activation and secretion. The property of adhesiveness for normal platelets requires a protein on the surface of the platelet membrane, known as glycoprotein Ib, to bind von Willebrand factor, a large multimeric plasma protein released from the alpha granules. Von Willebrand factor, when bound to glycoprotein Ib on the platelet surface, facilitates the interaction of platelets with a variety of other surfaces (e.g., the damaged vessel lining).

Platelet aggregation is the property of platelets to clump with each other to form a platelet plug. Two proteins on the platelet membrane play an important role in platelet aggregation: glycoprotein IIb and glycoprotein IIIa. These proteins form a complex in the membrane and expose a receptor site after platelet activation that binds fibrinogen (a bivalent molecule with two symmetrical halves that is found in relatively high concentration in plasma). Fibrinogen can bind simultaneously to two platelets. Thus, fibrinogen links platelets together (aggregation) through the glycoprotein IIb–IIIa complex that serves as the fibrinogen receptor.

Injury to the vessel lining and contact of the blood with tissues outside the vessel stimulates thrombin production by activating the clotting system. Thrombin causes platelet aggregation. Platelets exposed to thrombin secrete their granules and release the contents of these granules into the surrounding plasma.

Blood Coagulation

Coagulation is the replacement of a relatively unstable platelet plug with a stronger, more resilient blood clot through a series of interdependent, enzyme-mediated reactions that bring about the generation of thrombin and the formation of fibrin from fibrinogen. Coagulation is a sequential process that involves the interaction of numerous blood-clotting components called coagulation factors. There are 13 principal coagulation factors in all, and each has been assigned a Roman numeral, I to XIII.

Coagulation can be initiated through the activation of two separate pathways, designated extrinsic and intrinsic. These pathways are involved in regulating coagulation, and each is activated by a different trigger. Both pathways result in the production of factor X. The activation of this factor marks the beginning of the so-called common pathway of coagulation, which results in the formation of a clot.

The Intrinsic Pathway of Blood Coagulation

All the components necessary for the clotting process to proceed are found in the blood. As such, the proteins required for such clotting to take place are part of the intrinsic pathway of coagulation. This pathway involves a series of proteins, protein cofactors, and enzymes, which interact in reactions that take place on membrane surfaces. These reactions are initiated by tissue injury and result in the formation of a fibrin clot.

The intrinsic pathway is initiated by the activation of factor XII (Hageman factor) by certain negatively charged surfaces, including glass. High-molecular-weight kininogen and prekallikrein are two proteins that facilitate this activation. The enzyme form of factor XII (factor XIIa) catalyzes the conversion of factor XI to its enzyme form (factor XIa). Factor XIa catalyzes the conversion of factor IX to the activated form, factor IXa, in a reaction that requires calcium ions. Factor IXa assembles on the surface of membranes in complex with factor VIII. The factor IXa–factor VIII complex requires calcium to stabilize certain structures on these proteins associated with their membrane-binding properties. Factor X binds to the factor IXa–factor VIII complex and is activated to factor Xa. Factor Xa forms a complex with factor V on membrane surfaces in a reaction that also requires calcium ions. Prothrombin binds to the factor Xa–factor V complex and is converted to thrombin, which then cleaves fibrinogen (factor I) to fibrin (factor Ia), a monomer. The monomer fibrin molecules then link together (polymerize) to form long fibres, thereby forming a mesh that traps platelets, blood cells, and plasma.

Additional bonding between the units of the polymer is promoted by an enzyme known as factor XIIIa, which stabilizes the newly formed clot by cross-linkages. The fibrin meshwork then begins to contract, squeezing out its fluid contents. This process, called clot retraction, is the final step in coagulation. It yields a resilient, insoluble clot that can withstand the friction of blood flow. The cascade, or waterfall, effect of coagulation offers the possibility for amplification of a small signal associated with tissue injury into a major biologic event—the formation of a fibrin clot. Furthermore, careful regulation of this system is possible with the participation of two protein cofactors, factor VIII and factor V.

Certain negatively charged surfaces, including glass, kaolin, some synthetic plastics, and fabrics, activate factor XII to its enzyme form, factor XIIa. In contrast, certain materials have little tendency to activate factor XII. Inactive surfaces include some oils, waxes, resins, silicones, a few plastics, and endothelial cells, the most inert surface of all. The physicochemical properties that determine activity are unknown. The problem is important, because modern surgery requires a perfectly inactive material to make substitutes (prostheses) for heart valves and sections of blood vessels. The formation of clots (thrombi) on these surfaces can lead to serious or even fatal complications. Open-heart surgery requires pumping of blood through equipment that does not significantly activate the blood-clotting process. Similarly, blood filtration of waste products during kidney dialysis must not lead to the generation of fibrin clots. To minimize the activation of blood coagulation when blood flows over foreign surfaces, special drugs (anticoagulants) such as heparin are employed.

The activity of the intrinsic pathway may be assessed in a simple laboratory test called the partial thromboplastin time (PTT), or, more accurately, the activated partial thromboplastin time. Plasma is collected and anticoagulated with citrate buffer; the citrate binds and effectively removes functional calcium ions from the plasma. Under these conditions, a fibrin clot cannot be generated. A negatively charged material, such as the diatomaceous material kaolin, is added to the plasma. Kaolin activates factor XII to its enzyme form, factor XIIa, which then activates factor XI. The process is blocked from further activation because of the lack of calcium ions, which are required for the next reaction, the activation of factor IX. Upon the addition of calcium ions and a phospholipid preparation (which serves as an artificial membrane for the assembly of the blood-clotting protein complexes), the duration of time is recorded until a visible clot is formed. This reaction takes place in a matter of 25 to 50 seconds, depending upon the formulation of chemicals used. In practice, the clotting time of a test plasma is compared to the clotting time of normal plasma. Delayed clotting, measured as a prolonged partial thromboplastin time, may be caused by a deficiency in the activity of one or more of the blood-clotting factors or to a chemical inhibitor of blood coagulation.

The Extrinsic Pathway of Blood Coagulation

The extrinsic pathway is generally the first pathway activated in the coagulation process and is stimulated in response to a protein called tissue factor (or tissue thromboplastin). Tissue factor is found in many cells of the body but is particularly abundant in those of the brain, lungs, and placenta. Thus, tissue factor is expressed by cells that are normally found external to blood vessels. When a blood vessel breaks and these cells come into contact with blood, tissue factor activates factor VII, forming factor VIIa, which triggers a cascade of reactions that result in the rapid production of factor X.

Once activated, factor X proceeds to convert prothrombin to thrombin, which in turn catalyzes the conversion of fibrinogen into fibrin. With the exception of factor VII, all components of the extrinsic pathway are also components of the intrinsic pathway. As a result, components of the intrinsic pathway also may be activated by the extrinsic pathway; for example, in addition to activating factor X, factor VIIa activates factor IX, a necessary component of the intrinsic pathway. Such cross-activation serves to amplify the coagulation process.

The activity of the extrinsic pathway may be assessed in the laboratory using a simple test known as the prothrombin time. Tissue extract, or tissue thromboplastin, is extracted from animal tissues rich in tissue factor. Anticoagulated with citrate buffer, plasma is allowed to clot with the simultaneous addition of phospholipid, calcium, and thromboplastin. The duration of time until clot formation, known as the prothrombin time, is usually between 10 and 12 seconds. In practice, the clotting time of a test plasma is compared to the clotting time of normal plasma. Delayed clotting, measured as a prolonged prothrombin time, may be caused by a deficiency in the activity of one or more of the blood-clotting factors in the extrinsic pathway or to a chemical inhibitor of blood coagulation that interferes with the extrinsic pathway.

In summary, there are two independent mechanisms for initiating blood coagulation and for activating factor X: (1) negatively charged surfaces that initiate blood clotting through the intrinsic pathway (factors XII, XI, IX, and VIII), and (2) tissue factor on cells outside the blood that participates in the extrinsic pathway (factor VII). The common pathway (factor X, factor V, prothrombin, and fibrinogen) is shared by both systems. Although both pathways provide the opportunity to acquire meaningful information about clotting proteins using the partial thromboplastin time and the prothrombin time, it is most likely that the physiologically important pathway of blood coagulation is the extrinsic pathway initiated by tissue factor.

Biochemical Basis of Activation

The blood-clotting proteins circulate in the blood in their inactive, proenzyme form. The biochemical term for such proenzymes is zymogen. These zymogens are precursor enzymes that are converted to active enzymes by the cleavage of one or in some instances two peptide bonds. By splitting the protein into specific fragments, the zymogen is turned into an active enzyme that can itself split particular peptide bonds. This process, known generally as limited proteolysis, is equivalent to a molecular switch. By cutting a specific bond that connects two amino acids in the string of amino acids known as a polypeptide, an active enzyme is formed. Thus, the blood contains a system poised to become engaged instantaneously in the formation of blood clots if tissue is injured. Under normal conditions, however, blood clotting does not take place in the absence of tissue injury. The clotting proteins that function as zymogens in the blood include factor XII, factor XI, prekallikrein, factor IX, factor X, factor VII, and prothrombin.

Protein cofactors also play an important role in blood coagulation. Two protein cofactors, factor V and factor VIII, are large proteins that probably regulate blood coagulation. These proteins circulate in the blood as inactive cofactors. By the process of limited proteolysis, in which several cuts in the polypeptide chains of these cofactors are formed by the enzyme thrombin, factors V and VIII are converted to active cofactors. Factor V and factor VIII bind to membrane surfaces and form a focal point for the organization of certain protein complexes.

Inhibition of Clotting

After the activation of the blood-clotting system, the active enzymes must be turned off and the clotting process contained locally to the area of tissue injury. The details of the regulation of blood coagulation remain obscure, but it is clear that a series of blood proteins play a specialized role in disengaging the activated blood-clotting system. Antithrombin III is a plasma protein that combines with thrombin as well as most of the other activated blood-clotting proteins (e.g., factors Xa and IXa) to form inert complexes. This action is greatly enhanced by the presence of heparin, a substance formed by mast cells of the connective tissue. The hereditary deficiency of antithrombin III is associated with an excessive tendency toward clot formation, and manifestations of this defect are recurrent thrombophlebitis and pulmonary embolism. Heparin cofactor II is another plasma protease inhibitor that specifically forms a complex with thrombin, thus inactivating this enzyme. Protein C, a vitamin K-dependent protein, is a zymogen that requires vitamin K for its activation by thrombin complexed to thrombomodulin, a protein on the endothelial cell membrane. Activated protein C is capable of inactivating the active cofactor forms of factors VIII and V. Its action is enhanced when bound to protein S, a vitamin K-dependent protein that is attached to cell membranes (platelet or possibly endothelial cells). A deficiency in the level of protein C or protein S is associated with an excessive tendency to form clots.

Another anticoagulant effect is the fibrinolytic (fibrinsplitting) action of plasmin, an enzyme that catalyzes the removal of old fibrin at injury sites, which may be deposited in normal vessels. Plasmin is derived from plasminogen, an inert protein precursor that can be activated by tissue plasminogen activator. Streptokinase, urokinase, and tissue plasminogen activator are drugs that activate plasminogen and lead to the dissolution of clots.

Vitamin K and the Synthesis of Blood-Clotting Proteins

Most blood coagulation proteins are synthesized in the liver. In addition, factor VIII is synthesized in a large number of other tissues. One of the most important factors involved in clotting-protein synthesis is vitamin K (from the Danish word *koagulation*), which consists of any of several fat-soluble naphthoquinone compounds. Discovered in 1929, vitamin K was isolated and analyzed structurally in 1939 by Danish biochemist Henrik Dam.

There are several known forms of vitamin K, including a form called phylloquinone (vitamin K_1), which is synthesized by plants. A second form of vitamin K known as menaquinone (vitamin K_2) is synthesized by bacteria, including bacteria in the intestines of mammals. These bacteria produce most of the vitamin K that mammals require. A synthetic vitamin K precursor called menadione (vitamin K_3) is used as a vitamin supplement.

Vitamin K is required for the complete synthesis of six blood clotting factors: prothrombin, factor VII, factor IX, factor X, protein C, and protein S. These proteins are synthesized in precursor form. In a region of the liver cell called the rough endoplasmic reticulum, specific glutamic acid residues in the proteins that eventually give rise to these clotting factors are changed by an enzyme-mediated reaction to form a modified glutamic acid known as γ-carboxyglutamic acid. This enzyme reaction, known as γ-carboxylation, requires vitamin K as a cofactor. γ-Carboxyglutamic acid is a unique amino acid that binds to calcium. In the protein, γ-carboxyglutamic acids form the calcium-binding sites that characterize this form of calcium-binding protein, the vitamin K-dependent proteins. Calcium stabilizes certain structural forms of the vitamin K-dependent proteins, enabling these proteins to bind to cell membranes.

In the absence of vitamin K or in the presence of vitamin K antagonists such as warfarin, γ-carboxylation is inhibited and proteins are synthesized that are deficient in γ-carboxyglutamic acid. These proteins have no biologic activity because they do not bind to calcium or interact with membrane surfaces. Thus, a deficiency of vitamin K in the body leads to increased clotting time of the blood. Vitamin K deficiency is seldom naturally encountered in higher animals because the vitamin is usually adequately supplied in the diet, besides being synthesized by intestinal bacteria. In humans, deficiency may occur following the administration of certain drugs that inhibit the growth of the vitamin-synthesizing bacteria or as a result of disorders affecting the production or flow of bile, which itself is necessary for the intestinal absorption of vitamin K. In newborn infants, the absence of intestinal bacteria, low levels of vitamin K in the mother's milk, or the absence of body stores of vitamin K may result in bleeding, which can be prevented by the administration of vitamin K to the infant shortly after birth.

CHAPTER 3

BLOOD GROUP SYSTEMS

In 1901 scientists discovered the first blood groups—those of the ABO system. Since then, the realization that red blood cells possess proteins that can be used to classify them into various blood groups has revolutionized medicine. Prior to this knowledge, blood transfusions were dangerous and had unpredictable outcomes, with some patients experiencing severe reactions and others faring well for unknown reasons. Today, however, because blood group proteins on red cells can be identified accurately and because donor blood is screened for the presence of potentially dangerous infectious organisms, blood transfusions are relatively safe and effective procedures.

More than 20 blood group systems have been identified, each of which is genetically distinct. In fact, investigation of the genetic characteristics of blood groups has played a crucial role in improving knowledge of the underlying physiological functions of blood group proteins. This in turn led to the discovery that some of these substances have important roles in protection against diseases such as malaria. In the 20th century, some studies of blood groups focused solely on elucidating the incidence of blood group antigens in various populations worldwide. As a result, today there is extensive information available about the genetic frequency and prevalence of certain blood groups in populations of differing geographic, racial, or ethnic backgrounds. Thus, many blood groups serve as important genetic markers, providing key information about human populations and their evolution.

BLOOD GROUPS

The classification of blood is based on inherited differences (polymorphisms) in antigens on the surfaces of the red blood cells (erythrocytes). Inherited differences of white blood cells (leukocytes), platelets (thrombocytes), and plasma proteins also constitute blood groups.

HISTORICAL BACKGROUND

English physician William Harvey announced his observations on the circulation of the blood in 1616 and in 1628 published his famous monograph, *Exercitatio Anatomica de Motu Cordis et Sanguinis in Animalibus* (*The Anatomical Exercises Concerning the Motion of the Heart and Blood in Animals*). His discovery, that blood circulates around the body in a closed system, was an essential prerequisite of the concept of transfusing blood from one animal to another of the same or different species.

In England, experiments on the transfusion of blood were pioneered in dogs in 1665 by physician Richard Lower. In November 1667 Lower transfused the blood of a lamb into a man. Meanwhile, in France, Jean-Baptiste Denis, court physician to King Louis XIV, had also been transfusing lambs' blood into human subjects and described what is probably the first recorded account of the signs and symptoms of a hemolytic transfusion reaction. Denis was arrested after a fatality, and the procedure of transfusing the blood of other animals into humans was prohibited, by an act of the Chamber of Deputies in 1668, unless sanctioned by the Faculty of Medicine of Paris. Ten years later, the British Parliament also prohibited transfusions. Little advance was made in the next 150 years.

In England in the 19th century, interest was reawakened by the activities of obstetrician James Blundell, whose humanitarian instincts had been aroused by the frequently fatal outcome of hemorrhage occurring after childbirth. He insisted that it was better to use human blood for transfusion in such cases.

In 1875 German physiologist Leonard Landois showed that if the red blood cells of an animal belonging to one species are mixed with serum taken from an animal of another species, the red cells usually clump and sometimes burst (i.e., hemolyze). He attributed the appearance of black urine after transfusion of heterologous blood (blood from a different species) to the hemolysis of the incompatible red cells. Thus, the dangers of transfusing blood of another species to humans were established scientifically.

The human ABO blood groups were discovered by Austrian-born American biologist Karl Landsteiner in 1901. Landsteiner found that there are substances in the blood, antigens and antibodies, that induce clumping of red cells when red cells of one type are added to those of a second type. He recognized three groups—A, B, and O—based on their reactions to each other. A fourth group, AB, was identified a year later by another research team. Red cells of the A group clump with donor blood of the B group. Those of the B group clump with blood of the A group. Red cells of the AB group clump with those of the A or the B group because AB cells contain both A and B antigens. Finally, those of the O group do not generally clump with any group, because they do not contain A or B antigens. The application of knowledge of the ABO system in blood transfusion practice is of enormous importance, because mistakes can have fatal consequences.

Austrian-born pathologist Karl Landsteiner, c. 1920. Landsteiner won the Nobel Prize for his discovery of the human ABO blood-group system. He also had a hand in the discovery of the Rh system. Keystone/Hulton Archive/ Getty Images

The discovery of the Rh system was made by Landsteiner and Alexander Wiener in 1940. They tested human red cells with antisera developed in rabbits and guinea pigs by immunization of the animals with the red cells of the rhesus monkey *Macaca mulatta*.

Other blood groups were identified later, such as Kell, Diego, Lutheran, Duffy, and Kidd. The remaining blood group systems were first described after antibodies were identified in patients. Frequently, such discoveries resulted from the search for the explanation of an unexpected unfavourable reaction in a recipient after a transfusion with formerly compatible blood. In such cases the antibodies in the recipient were produced against previously unidentified antigens in the donor's blood. For example, in the case of the Rh system, the presence of antibodies in the maternal serum directed against antigens present on the red cells of the fetus can have serious consequences because of antigen–antibody reactions that produce erythroblastosis fetalis, or hemolytic disease of the newborn. This condition, which is potentially fatal to the fetus, results in severe fetal anemia because the maternal antibodies destroy the fetal red blood cells. Some of the other blood group systems—for example, the Kell and Kidd systems—were discovered because an infant was found to have erythroblastosis fetalis even though mother and fetus were compatible as far as the Rh system was concerned.

BLOOD TYPING

The classification of blood in terms of distinctive inherited characteristics that are associated with the antigens located on the surface of red blood cells is known as blood typing. The ABO and the Rh blood groups are among those most commonly considered. Identification of these determinants has become indispensable in connection with blood transfusion, because the recipient and donor must have the same, or compatible, blood groups. Otherwise, hemolysis (destruction) or coagulation (clotting) results from interaction of an antigen on the red blood cells of one with an antibody in the serum of the other. In addition, blood typing serves to promptly identify the cause of such disorders as erythroblastosis fetalis. Because blood group determinants are inherited according to generally known mechanisms of heredity, blood typing sometimes provides a method for resolving cases of disputed paternity.

ABO BLOOD GROUP SYSTEM

The ABO blood group system is the classification of human blood based on the inherited properties of red blood cells as determined by the presence or absence of the antigens A and B, which are carried on the surface of the red cells. Persons may thus have type A, type B, type O, or type AB blood. The A, B, and O blood groups were first identified by Austrian immunologist Karl Landsteiner in 1901.

Blood containing red cells with type A antigen on their surface has in its serum (fluid) antibodies against type B red cells. If, in transfusion, type B blood is injected into persons with type A blood, the red cells in the injected blood will be destroyed by the antibodies in the recipient's blood. In the same way, type A red cells will be destroyed by anti-A antibodies in type B blood. Type O blood can be injected into persons with type A, B, or O blood unless there is incompatibility with respect to some other blood group system also present. Persons with type AB blood can receive type A, B, or O blood. (See p. 227 for a table of the ABO and RH groups in transfusion.)

Blood group O is the most common blood type throughout the world, particularly among peoples of South and Central America. Type B is prevalent in Asia, especially in northern India. Type A also is common all over the world; the highest frequency is among the Blackfoot Indians of Montana and the Sami people of northern Scandinavia.

The ABO antigens are developed well before birth and remain throughout life. Children acquire ABO antibodies passively from their mother before birth, but by three months infants are making their own—it is believed the stimulus for such antibody formation is from contact with ABO-like antigenic substances in nature. Erythroblastosis fetalis involving A, B, or O antigens is rare and occurs in only a small percentage of cases in which a mother is type O and a fetus is either type A or type B.

MNSs BLOOD GROUP SYSTEM

The MNSs blood group system is the classification of human blood based on the presence of various substances known as M, N, S, and s antigens on the surfaces of red blood cells. This system, first discovered in 1927, has many distinct phenotypes and is of interest in genetic and anthropological studies of human populations.

There are more than 40 antigens in the MNSs blood group system. These antigens are encoded by two highly polymorphic (variable) genes, known as *GYPA* and *GYPB* (glycophorin A and B, respectively). The system consists of two pairs of codominant alleles (alternative forms of a gene), designated *M* and *N* (identified in 1927) and *S* and *s* (identified 1947 and 1951, respectively). The alleles *M* and *N* are usually distributed in populations in approximately equal frequencies. However, the *S* and *s* alleles have varying frequencies, with the *S* allele occurring in about 55 percent of Caucasians and 30 percent of African Americans, and the *s* allele occurring in roughly 90 percent of individuals in both populations.

Several phenotypes in the MNSs antigen system result from deletion mutations in the *GYPA* and *GYPB* genes. Examples of these phenotypes include S-s-U-, En(a-), and Mk. Some antigens, including He (Henshaw, identified in 1951), Dantu, St^a (Stone), and Mi^a (Miltenberger), are formed by genetic recombination (the exchange of genetic material between genes) of *GYPA* and *GYPB*.

Antibodies to the M and N antigens rarely cause incompatibility reactions. However, antibodies to S, s, and several other antigens, including En^a and Mi^a, can cause transfusion reactions and erythroblastosis fetalis.

P BLOOD GROUP SYSTEM

The P blood group system is the classification of human blood based on the presence of any of three substances known as the P, P$_1$, and P^k antigens on the surfaces of red blood cells. These antigens are also expressed on the surfaces of cells lining the urinary tract, where they have been identified as adhesion sites for *Escherichia coli* bacteria, which cause urinary tract infections.

Genetically, the P blood group, which was discovered in 1927, consists of alleles designated *P*, *P$_1$*, and *P^k*. The P and P$_1$ antigens are synthesized by an enzyme encoded by a gene known as *B3GALNT1* (beta-1,3-N-acetylgalactosaminyltransferase 1), whereas the P^k antigen is synthesized by an enzyme encoded by a gene called *A4GALT* (alpha 1,4-galactosyltransferase).

There are five phenotypes in the P blood group system: P$_1$, P$_2$, P$_1^k$, P$_2^k$, and p, formerly designated Tj(a-). The most commonly occurring of these is the P$_1$ phenotype, which displays all three P antigens. The P$_2$ phenotype consists of the P and P^k antigens and is the second most common phenotype in the P system. In contrast, the phenotypes P$_1^k$ (P$_1$ and P^k antigens), P$_2^k$ (P^k antigen only), and p (no antigens) are extremely uncommon.

Antibodies against P, P$_1$, and P^k antigens can cause transfusion reactions. Antibodies against P and P^k antigens may cause severe erythroblastosis fetalis or spontaneous abortion.

Rh Blood Group System

The Rh blood group system is the classification of blood according to the presence or absence of the Rh antigen, often called the Rh factor, on the cell membranes of the red blood cells. The designation Rh is derived from the use of the blood of rhesus monkeys in the basic test for determining the presence of the Rh antigen in human blood. Since the Rh blood group system was discovered in 1940, many distinct Rh antigens have been identified, but the first and most common one, called RhD, causes the most severe immune reaction and is the primary determinant of the Rh trait.

The Rh antigen poses a danger for the Rh-negative person, who lacks the antigen, if Rh-positive blood is given in transfusion. Adverse effects may not occur the first time Rh-incompatible blood is given, but the immune system responds to the foreign Rh antigen by producing anti-Rh antibodies. If Rh-positive blood is given again after the antibodies form, they will attack the foreign red blood cells, causing them to clump together, or agglutinate. The resulting hemolysis, or destruction of the red blood cells, causes serious illness and sometimes death.

A similar hazard exists during pregnancy for the Rh-positive offspring of Rh-incompatible parents, when the mother is Rh-negative and the father is Rh-positive. The first child of such parents is usually in no danger unless the mother has acquired anti-Rh antibodies by virtue of incompatible blood transfusion. During labour, however, a small amount of the fetus's blood may enter the

A gathering in the streets of the Basque city of Bilbao. The highest concentration of blood with an Rh-negative factor, which is relatively rare, occurs among the Basques. Rafa Rivas/AFP/Getty Images

mother's bloodstream. The mother will then produce anti-Rh antibodies, which will attack any Rh-incompatible fetus in subsequent pregnancies. This process produces erythroblastosis fetalis. Treatment of erythroblastosis fetalis usually entails one or more exchange transfusions. The disease can be avoided by vaccinating the mother with Rh immunoglobulin after delivery of her firstborn if there is Rh-incompatibility. The Rh vaccine destroys any fetal blood cells before the mother's immune system can develop antibodies.

Although the Rh-negative trait is rare in most parts of the world, it occurs in about 15 percent of Caucasians in Europe, Canada, and the United States. The trait's highest incidence is among the Basques of the Pyrenees (25–35 percent) and the Imazighen (Berbers) of Africa and the Bedouins of the Sinai Peninsula (18–30 percent).

LUTHERAN BLOOD GROUP SYSTEM

The Lutheran blood group system is the classification of human blood based on the presence of substances called Lutheran antigens on the surfaces of red blood cells. There are 19 known Lutheran antigens, all of which arise from variations in a gene called *BCAM* (basal cell adhesion molecule). The system is based on the expression of two codominant alleles, designated Lu^a and Lu^b. The antigens Au^a and Au^b, known as the Auberger antigens, were once thought to make up a separate blood group but were later shown to be Lutheran antigens arising from variations in the *BCAM* gene.

The phenotypes Lu(a+b-) and Lu(a+b+) are found at various frequencies within populations. The Lu(a-b+) phenotype is the most common in all populations, whereas the Lu(a-b-) phenotype is extremely uncommon. Although present in the fetus, Lu^a is seldom the cause of erythroblastosis fetalis or of transfusion reactions.

KELL BLOOD GROUP SYSTEM

The Kell blood group system is the classification of human blood based on the presence on the surfaces of red blood cells of various antigens encoded by the *KEL* gene. The system, discovered in 1946, is characterized by a high degree of polymorphism (genetic variation), and thus studies of the Kell antigens have provided insight into the development of polymorphic traits in the context of human evolution. Antibodies generated against antigens in the Kell system can cause transfusion reactions and erythroblastosis fetalis. After the Rh and ABO systems, the Kell system is the third most common blood group to cause these reactions.

In total, there are 25 Kell antigens, all of which are encoded by the *KEL* gene. The two primary, codominant alleles of the *KEL* gene include *K* and *k*, which encode the K (Kell) and k (Cellano) antigens, respectively. The k antigen is common, occurring in more than 90 percent of African Americans and Caucasians. Polymorphisms in the *KEL* gene give rise to different antigens, including the Js^a and Js^b antigens. The Js^b antigen is found in 100 percent of Caucasians and 80 percent of African Americans. Examples of other Kell antigens include Kp^a (Penney) and Kp^b (Rautenberg).

Kell antigens normally associate with a protein called Kx on the surfaces of red blood cells. In some people, the Kx protein is absent, resulting in McLeod syndrome. Characteristics of this syndrome include acanthocytosis (thorny projections on red blood cells) and reduced Kell antigen expression. These abnormalities often lead to defects in muscle and nerve function that manifest as disordered movement, psychological disturbance, and loss of reflexes.

LEWIS BLOOD GROUP SYSTEM

The Lewis blood group system is the classification of human blood based on the expression of glycoproteins called Lewis (Le) antigens on the surfaces of red blood cells or in body fluids, or both. The Lewis antigen system is intimately associated with the secretor system and ABO blood group system biochemically, but the genetic loci are not linked.

The system consists of two alleles, designated *Le* (dominant) and *le*. The presence of *Le* specifies the formation of antigen Le^a (identified 1946), which is found on the red cells of 20 percent of Europeans and in the saliva and other fluids of more than 90 percent. Le^a is a water-soluble antigen. Red blood cells acquire Lewis specificity secondarily by adsorbing antigen onto their surfaces from blood plasma. A second antigen, Le^b (identified 1948), occurs only when alleles *Le* and *H* (a precursor of the ABO blood group system) interact. Le^b is found only in secretors and reaches a frequency of 70 percent in Europeans.

It has been proposed that Le^a is made from a "precursor substance" in the presence of allele *Le*. In the further presence of alleles *H* and *Se* (secretor system), Le^a substance is partially converted to H substance; antigens Le^a, Le^b, and H are isolable. With the subsequent action of alleles *A* or *B* or both, H substance is converted and the ABO blood types are expressed, both in the body fluids and on the red blood cells. Variations in the genes present in the individual explain the various combinations of expression of the Lewis, ABO, and secretor systems in the body.

Duffy Blood Group System

The Duffy blood group system is the classification of human blood based on the presence of glycoproteins known as Fy antigens on the surface of red blood cells, endothelial cells (cells lining the inner surface of blood vessels), and epithelial cells in the alveoli of the lungs and in the collecting tubules of the kidneys. The Duffy antigens Fy^a (Fy1) and Fy^b (Fy2) were discovered in 1950 and 1951, respectively.

The Duffy antigens act as receptors for substances called chemokines, which are hormonelike molecules that attract cells of the immune system to particular sites in the body. The Duffy antigens also serve as receptors for the malarial parasites *Plasmodium knowlesi* and *P. vivax*. There are four possible Fy phenotypes, which include Fy^{a+b+}, Fy^{a+b-}, Fy^{a-b+}, and Fy^{a-b-}. The Fy^{a+b+} phenotype is the most common in Caucasians, occurring in nearly 50 percent of the population. The phenotype Fy^{a+b-} occurs in some 90 percent of individuals of Chinese descent and in less than 20 percent of Caucasians, and the phenotype Fy^{a-b+} occurs in about 34 percent of Caucasians and 22 percent of African Americans. The phenotype Fy^{a-b-} occurs in nearly 70 percent of individuals of African descent and is rare in Caucasians. Because the Duffy antigens are not expressed in the Fy^{a-b-} phenotype, and hence there are no receptors to which malarial parasites can bind, the null condition is associated with some degree of protection against malaria. Research has indicated that the increased frequency of the Fy^{a-b-} phenotype in West Africans and other individuals of African descent is the result of natural selection for disease resistance.

The Duffy antigens arise from variations in a gene known as *DARC*, which encodes the chemokine receptor protein found on the surfaces of Duffy-expressing cells. Antibodies to Duffy antigens designated Fy3 through Fy5 were discovered in the early 1970s, and in the following decade, antibodies to another antigen, Fy6, were discovered. The Fy3 through Fy6 antigens represent variations in the Fy^a and Fy^b epitopes, which are the portions of antigens that are capable of stimulating immune responses.

Duffy antigens also have been found on the surfaces of Purkinje cells in the brain and on cells of the colon, spleen, and thyroid gland. Antibodies to the Duffy antigens have been associated with transfusion reactions and with erythroblastosis fetalis.

KIDD BLOOD GROUP SYSTEM

The Kidd blood group system is the classification of human blood based on the presence of glycoproteins known as Kidd (Jk) antigens on the surfaces of red blood cells. The Kidd glycoprotein functions to maintain the osmotic stability of red blood cells by acting as a transporter of urea. Antibodies that bind to the Kidd proteins can cause delayed transfusion reactions and erythroblastosis fetalis.

The Kidd blood group system, discovered in 1951, consists of three known antigens, designated Jk^a, Jk^b, and Jk3, all of which are encoded by a gene known as *SLC14A1* (solute carrier family 14, member 1). The Jk^a antigen occurs in more than 90 percent of African Americans, 75 percent of Caucasians, and 70 percent of Asians. The Jk^b antigen is found in about 75 percent of Caucasians and Asians and approximately 50 percent of African Americans. The Jk3 antigen occurs in nearly 100 percent of all populations, and thus, antibodies against Jk3 are rare. The absence of both Jk^a and Jk^b antigens, designated phenotypically as Jk(a-b-), is infrequent, but it is found in roughly 1 percent of Polynesians. The most common Kidd phenotype is Jk(a+b+), which occurs in about 50 percent of Caucasians and Asians and about 40 percent of African Americans.

DIEGO BLOOD GROUP SYSTEM

The Diego blood group system is the classification of human blood according to the properties conferred by the presence of an antigen designated Di. Although there are 21 known Diego antigens, the determination of an individual's Diego blood type is based on the antigens denoted Di^a (identified in 1955) and Di^b (identified in 1967). The Diego blood group system is associated with a gene known as *SLC4A1* (solute carrier family 4, anion exchanger, member 1). This gene encodes a substance called band 3 protein, which is expressed on the surface of red blood cells and plays a central role in mediating the transport of carbon dioxide in the blood. Although mutations in *SLC4A1* can give rise to diseases such as hereditary ovalocytosis (a disease in which red blood cells are oval shaped, not round), a number of other mutations result in the production of Diego antigens.

The Di^a antigen is found in more than 35 percent of South American Indians and about 12 percent of people of Chinese and Japanese descent. Diego incompatibility of mother and fetus can cause erythroblastosis fetalis.

YT BLOOD GROUP SYSTEM

The Yt blood group system (also known as the Cartwright blood group system) is the classification of human blood based on the presence of molecules known as Yt antigens on the surface of red blood cells. The Yt antigens, Yt^a and Yt^b, were discovered in 1956 and 1964, respectively. The importance of the Yt blood group in humans was revealed in the 1990s, when researchers uncovered the molecular differences between the two Yt antigens and associated the absence of these antigens from red blood cells with a disease known as paroxysmal nocturnal hemoglobinuria.

The Yt antigens are located on a glycosylphosphatidylinositol (GPI)-anchored protein that is encoded by the gene *ACHE* (acetylcholinesterase). The Yt^a and Yt^b antigens are distinguished molecularly by a single amino acid difference in the acetylcholinesterase protein. Acetylcholinesterase normally acts as an enzyme in the nervous system, rendering a neurotransmitter called acetylcholine inactive in the gaps (synapses) between neurons. However, the precise function of acetylcholinesterase on red blood cells is unclear. The Yt^a antigen occurs in about 99 percent of individuals in nearly all populations. In contrast, the Yt^b antigen typically has an incidence of about 8 percent, but it is more frequent in certain populations (e.g., it is found in about 20 percent of Israelis).

In healthy individuals, the Yt antigen null phenotype, in which both antigens are absent from the surface of red blood cells, designated Yt(a-b-), has not been detected. However, in persons affected by paroxysmal nocturnal hemoglobinuria, in which red blood cells are destroyed by cells of the immune system, GPI-linked proteins are absent, and hence the Yt antigens are also typically missing from cells (in some cases, the antigens may be very weakly expressed). The absence of GPI-linked proteins is suspected to play a role in facilitating the premature destruction of red blood cells. Antibodies to Yt antigens have been associated with delayed transfusion reactions.

Ii Blood Group System

The Ii blood group system is the classification of human blood based on the presence of antigens I and i on the surface of red blood cells. The Ii blood group system is associated with cold antibodies (antibodies that function only at temperatures below normal body heat) and several blood diseases.

The I antigen is found in the cell membrane of red blood cells in all adults, whereas the i antigen is found only on red blood cells of the developing fetus and newborn infants. In newborn infants, the i antigen undergoes gradual conversion to reach adult levels of the I antigen within 18 months of birth. The formation of the I antigen from the i antigen in red blood cells is catalyzed by a protein called I-branching enzyme. Rare variants of the i antigen exist. For example, the antigen i_I is found as a rarity in Caucasians, and the antigen i_2 is found as a rarity mostly among African Americans. Natural antibodies to I are found in adults who possess the i antigen. The presence of the i antigen in adults is caused by mutation of a gene known as *GCNT2*, which encodes the I-branching enzyme.

Auto-antibodies to I are the commonest source of cold antibodies in acquired hemolytic anemia. Auto-antibodies to i have been identified in persons with leukemia and other blood diseases; a transient auto-anti-i is relatively common in people with infectious mononucleosis.

XG BLOOD GROUP SYSTEM

The Xg blood group system is the classification of human blood based on the presence of proteins called Xg antigens on the surfaces of red blood cells. The Xg blood group system is the only blood group in which the antigen-encoding genes are located on the X chromosome. Discovery of the system in 1962 greatly helped map the X chromosome.

The group consists of one identifiable antigen, Xg^a; two phenotypes, Xg(a+) and Xg(a-); and a pair of alleles, *Xg^a*, which is dominant to *Xg*. This blood group follows the pattern for sex-chromosome inheritance: daughters may receive a gene for Xg^a from either the mother or the father, but sons may inherit Xg^a only from the mother. The frequency of Xg(a+) in Caucasian males is about 65 percent and in Caucasian females is approximately 90 percent. Distribution in other populations remains unclear, but Asians and African Americans appear to have low frequencies of Xg^a. The antigen is developed at birth but does not readily induce the development of antibodies.

DOMBROCK BLOOD GROUP SYSTEM

The Dombrock blood group system is the classification of human blood based on the presence of certain glycoproteins, originally only the so-called Do antigens, on the surface of red blood cells. Antibodies to the Dombrock antigen Do^a were discovered in 1965 in a patient who had received a blood transfusion. In 1973 a second Dombrock antigen, Do^b, was identified. The Dombrock blood group was expanded in the 1990s to include three other antigens, Gy^a (Gregory antigen), Hy (Holley antigen), and Jo^a (Joseph antigen), that occur on the same protein as the Do antigens.

The Dombrock antigens are located on a glycosylphosphatidylinositol (GPI)-anchored protein that is encoded by the gene *ART4* (ADP-ribosyltransferase 4). The GPI is embedded in the membrane of Dombrock-expressing cells, thereby enabling the protein and its antigen-containing residue to remain exposed on the outside surface of the cells. Genetic variations in *ART4* that result in an altered amino acid sequence of the encoded protein give rise to the different Dombrock antigens. The Do^b antigen is distinguished from the Do^a antigen in that it contains an amino acid sequence known as an arginine-glycine-aspartic acid (RGD) motif, which is known to play a role in cell-to-cell interactions.

Studies have indicated that about 65 percent of northern Europeans carry the Do^a antigen and that the Do^b antigen has an increased incidence in Africans and Asians. In all populations studied, the Gy^a, Hy, and Jo^a antigens have been estimated to occur in more than 99 percent of individuals. In addition to the expression of the Do^a antigen on circulating red blood cells, it is found on lymphocytes; on lymph nodes; in bone marrow; and in the tissues of the spleen, ovaries, testes, intestines, and fetal heart. The expression of Dombrock antigens is highest in the fetal liver. In rare cases, none of the five Dombrock antigens are expressed on red blood cells, resulting in a Dombrock-null phenotype.

Antibodies to Dombrock antigens have been associated with severe transfusion reactions. In addition, the absence of Dombrock antigens can occur as a result of the loss of GPI-anchored proteins from the surface of red blood cells. The loss of these proteins underlies an infrequent condition known as paroxysmal nocturnal hemoglobinuria, in which red blood cells undergo premature destruction by immune cells.

SECRETOR SYSTEM

The secretor system is a phenotype based on the presence of soluble antigens on the surfaces of red blood cells and in body fluids, including saliva, semen, sweat, and gastrointestinal juices. The ability to secrete antigens into body fluids is important in medicine and genetics because of its association with immune system function and its association with other blood groups, including the Lewis and ABO blood group systems.

In most populations, nearly 80 percent of individuals are secretors. It is believed that the presence of water-soluble antigens in the tissues, particularly in the gastrointestinal tract, is of some selective advantage. Attempts to correlate secretion with disease have shown that duodenal ulcers (especially in persons with blood type O) and possibly also rheumatic fever and polio are more common in nonsecretors than in secretors.

The secretor system consists of a pair of alleles, designated *Se* (dominant) and *se*, in genotypes *SeSe* and *Sese* (secretors), and *sese* (nonsecretors), making it a good example of a simple Mendelian genetic system. The secretor

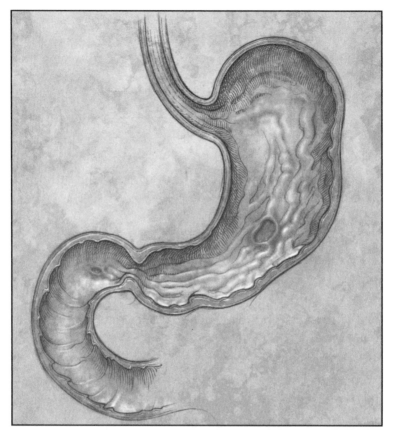

A medical depiction of ulcerations in the intestinal tract. Scientists suspect that the secretion of soluble antigens may help protect against duodenal ulcers and other diseases. Scott Bodell/Photodisc/Getty Images

system is intimately associated with the Lewis system biochemically and genetically. Antigens present in both the secretor and Lewis systems are encoded by a gene known as *FUT2* (fucosyltransferase 2).

ANTIGENS AND ANTIBODIES

The red cells of an individual contain antigens on their surfaces that correspond to their blood group and antibodies in the serum that identify and combine with the antigen sites on the surfaces of red cells of another type. The reaction between red cells and corresponding antibodies usually results in clumping (agglutination) of the red cells. Therefore, antigens on the surfaces of these red cells are often referred to as agglutinogens.

Antibodies are part of the circulating plasma proteins known as immunoglobulins, which are classified by molecular size and weight and by several other biochemical properties. Most blood group antibodies are found either on immunoglobulin G (IgG) or immunoglobulin M (IgM) molecules, but occasionally the immunoglobulin A (IgA) class may exhibit blood group specificity. Naturally occurring antibodies are the result of immunization by substances in nature that have structures similar to human blood groups. These antibodies are present in an individual despite the fact that there has been no previous exposure to the corresponding red cell antigens. For example, anti-A in the plasma of people of blood group B and anti-B in the plasma of people of blood group A. Immune antibodies are evoked by exposure to the corresponding red cell antigen.

Immunization (i.e., the production of antibodies in response to antigen) against blood group antigens in humans can occur as a result of pregnancy, blood transfusion, or deliberate immunization. The combination of pregnancy and transfusion is a particularly potent stimulus. Individual blood group antigens vary in their antigenic potential. For example, some antigens belonging to the Rh and ABO systems are strongly immunogenic (i.e., capable of inducing antibody formation), whereas the antigens of the Kidd and Duffy blood group systems are much weaker immunogens.

The blood group antigens are not restricted solely to red cells or even to hematopoietic tissues. The antigens of the ABO system are widely distributed throughout the tissues and have been unequivocally identified on platelets and white cells (both lymphocytes and polymorphonuclear leukocytes) and in skin, epithelial (lining) cells of the gastrointestinal tract, kidney, urinary tract, and lining of the blood vessels. Evidence for the presence of the antigens of other blood group systems on cells other than red cells is less well substantiated. Among the red cell antigens, only those of the ABO system are regarded as tissue antigens and therefore need to be considered in organ transplantation.

CHEMISTRY OF BLOOD GROUPS

The exact chemical structure of some blood groups has been identified, as have the gene products (i.e., those molecules synthesized as a result of an inherited genetic code on a gene of a chromosome) that assist in synthesizing the antigens on the red cell surface that determine the blood type. Blood group antigens are present on glycolipid and glycoprotein molecules of the red cell membrane. The carbohydrate chains of the membrane glycolipids are oriented toward the external surface of the red cell membrane and carry antigens of the ABO, Hh, Ii, and P systems. Glycoproteins, which traverse the red cell membrane, have a polypeptide backbone to which carbohydrates are attached. An abundant glycoprotein, band 3, contains ABO, Hh, and Ii antigens. Another integral membrane glycoprotein, glycophorin A, contains large numbers of sialic acid molecules and MN blood group structures; another, glycophorin B, contains Ss and U antigens.

The genes responsible for inheritance of ABH and Lewis antigens are glycosyltransferases (a group of enzymes that catalyze the addition of specific sugar residues to the core precursor substance). For example, the *H* gene codes for the production of a specific glycosyl-transferase that adds l-fucose to a core precursor substance, resulting in the H antigen. The *Le* gene codes for the production of a specific glycosyltransferase that adds l-fucose to the same core precursor substance, but in a different place, forming the Lewis antigen. The *A* gene adds *N*-acetyl-**d**-galactosamine (H must be present), forming the A antigen. Finally, the *B* gene adds **d**-galactose (H must be present), forming the B antigen. The P system is analogous to the ABH and Lewis blood groups in the sense that the P antigens are built by the addition of sugars to precursor globoside and paragloboside glycolipids, and the genes responsible for these antigens must produce glycosyltransferase enzymes.

The genes that code for MNSs glycoproteins change two amino acids in the sequence of the glycoprotein to account for different antigen specificities. Additional analysis of red cell membrane glycoproteins has shown that in some cases the absence of blood group antigens is associated with an absence of minor membrane glycoproteins that are present normally in antigen-positive persons.

BLOOD GROUPS AND GENETIC LINKAGE

Red cell groups act as markers (inherited characteristics) for genes present on chromosomes, which are responsible for their expression. The site of a particular genetic system on a chromosome is called a locus. Each locus may be the site of several alleles (alternative genes). In an ordinary cell of the human body, there are 46 chromosomes arranged in 23 pairs, 22 pairs of which are autosomes (chromosomes other than sex chromosomes), with the remaining pair being the sex chromosomes, designated

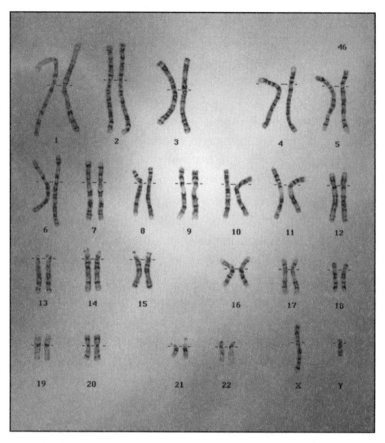

A magnified chromosome set. Because blood groups are an inherited trait that is carried by the sex chromosome, they can be used as genetic markers. Randy Allbritton/Photodisc/Getty Images

XX in females and XY in males. The loci of the blood group systems are on the autosomes, except for Xg, which is unique among the blood groups in being located on the X chromosome. Genes carried by the X chromosome are said to be sex-linked. Since the blood groups are inherited in a regular fashion, they can be used as genetic markers in family studies to investigate whether any two particular loci are sited on the same chromosome—i.e., are linked. The genes sited at loci on the same chromosome travel together from parent to child, and, if the loci are close together, the genes will rarely be separated.

Loci that are farther apart can be separated by recombination. This happens when material is exchanged between homologous chromosomes (pair of chromosomes) by crossing over during the process of cell division (mitosis). The reproductive cells contain half the number of chromosomes of the rest of the body. Ova carry an X chromosome and spermatozoa an X or a Y. The characteristic number of 46 chromosomes is restored at fertilization. In a classical pedigree linkage study, all family members are examined for a test character as well as for evidence of the nonindependent segregation of pairs of characters. The results must be assessed statistically to determine linkage. Individual chromosomes are identified by the banding patterns revealed by different staining techniques. Segments of chromosomes or chromosomes that are aberrant in number and morphology may be precisely identified. Other methods for localizing markers on chromosomes include somatic cell hybridization (cell culture with alignment of single strands of RNA and DNA) and use of DNA probes (strands of radiolabeled DNA). These methods are useful in classical linkage studies to locate blood group loci. The loci for many red cell groups have been found on chromosomes and in many cases have been further localized on a particular chromosome.

In some of the blood group systems, the amount of antigen produced depends on the genetic constitution. The ABO blood group gene codes for a specific carbohydrate transferase enzyme that catalyzes the addition of specific sugars onto a precursor substance. As a new sugar is added, a new antigen is produced. Antigens in the MNSs blood system are the products of genes that control terminal amino acid sequence. The amount of antigen present may depend on the amount of gene product inherited or on the activity of the gene product (i.e., transferase). The red cells of a person whose genotype is *MM* show more M antigen than do *MN* red cells. In the case of ABO, the same mechanism may also play a role in antigen expression, but specific activity of the inherited transferase may be more important.

The amount of antigen produced can also be influenced by the position of the genes. Such effects within a genetic complex can be caused by determinants on the same chromosome—they are then said to be cis—or by determinants on the opposite chromosome of a chromosome pair—trans.

In the Rh combination cdE/cde, more E antigen is produced than in the combination cDE/cde. This may be caused by the suppressor effect of D on E. An example of suppression in the trans situation is that more C antigen is detectable on the red cells from CDe/cde donors than on those of CDe/cDE people. The inheritance of the Rh system probably depends on the existence of operator genes, which turn the activity of closely linked structural genes on or off. The operator genes are themselves controlled by regulator genes. The operator genes are responsible for the quantity of Rh antigens, whereas the structural genes are responsible for their qualitative characteristics.

The detection of recombination (exchange of material between chromosomes) or mutation in human families is complicated by questions of paternity. In spite of the large number of families that have been studied, it is an extremely rare occurrence. The paucity of examples may indicate that the recombinant and mutation rate for blood group genes is lower than that estimated for other human genes.

BLOOD GROUPS AND
POPULATION GROUPS

The blood groups are found in all human populations but vary in frequency. An analysis of populations yields striking differences in the frequency of some blood group genes. The frequency of the *A* gene is the highest among Australian Aborigines, the Blackfoot Indians of Montana in the United States, and the Sami people of northern Scandinavia. The *O* gene is common throughout the world, particularly among peoples of South and Central America. The maximum frequency of the *B* gene occurs in Central Asia and northern India. On the Rh system most northern and central European populations differ from each other only slightly and are characterized by a *cde* (*r*) frequency of about 40 percent. Africans show a preponderance of the complex *cDe*, and the frequency of *cde* is about 20 percent. In eastern Asia *cde* is almost wholly absent, and, because everyone has the D antigen, erythroblastosis fetalis (caused by the presence of maternal anti-D) is unknown in these populations.

The blood group frequencies in small inbred populations reflect the influences of genetic drift. In a small community, an allele can be lost from the genetic pool if persons carrying it happen to be infertile, whereas it can increase in frequency if advantage exists. It has been suggested, for example, that *B* alleles were lost by chance from Native Americans and Australian Aborigines when these communities were small. There are pronounced discrepancies in blood group frequencies between the people of eastern Asia and the aboriginal peoples of the Americas. Other blood group frequencies in different populations show that ancestors might share some common attribute indicating a close resemblance between populations.

Nonhuman primates carry blood group antigens that can be detected with reagents used for typing humans. The closer their evolutionary relationship to humans, the greater their similarity with respect to antigens. The red cells of the apes, with the exception of the gorilla, have ABO antigens that are indistinguishable from those of human cells. Chimpanzees and orangutans are most frequently group A, but groups O, B, and AB are represented. Gibbons can be of any group except O, and gorillas have a B-like antigen that is not identical in activity with the human one. In both Old and New World monkeys, the red cells do not react with anti-A or with anti-B, but, when the secretions are examined, A and B substances and agglutinins are present in the serum. As far as the Rh system is concerned, chimpanzees carry two Rh antigens—D and c (hr′)—but not the others, whereas gibbons have only c (hr′). The red cells of monkeys do not give clear-cut reactions with human anti-Rh sera.

CHAPTER 4

BLOOD ANALYSIS AND THERAPEUTIC APPLICATIONS

Blood analysis is one of the most important steps in the accurate diagnosis of disease and in the monitoring of treatments and disease progression. A number of diseases involve biochemical or metabolic abnormalities that can be detected by specific blood tests, and hence a variety of laboratory blood tests exist for the diagnosis of specific diseases. Included among these are measurements of serum albumin, counts of the different types of blood cells, and identification of antigens and antibodies circulating in the blood, which may be indicative of bacterial, viral, or parasitic infection.

In addition to the diagnostic applications of blood analysis, several tests are also used therapeutically, for example, to match blood groups for transfusion and bone marrow transplantation and to match antigens for organ transplantation. They sometimes also are used for other purposes, such as paternity testing. Although there are many methods of blood analysis, these techniques are constantly being refined, and new approaches that are faster and more effective than traditional methods are under development.

BLOOD AND DISEASE

Long before the nature and composition of blood were known, a variety of symptoms were attributed to disordered blood. Red blood cells were not recognized until the

17th century, and it was another 100 years before one type of white blood cell, the lymphocyte, and blood clotting (coagulation) were described. In the 19th century, other forms of white cells were discovered, and a number of diseases of the blood and blood-forming organs were distinguished. Morphological changes—the changes in form and structure—that take place in the blood during disease and the signs and symptoms of the various blood diseases were described in the 19th century and the first quarter of the 20th century. In the years that followed, a more physiological approach began to develop, concerned with the mechanisms underlying the development of a variety of diseases and with the ways in which abnormalities might be corrected.

Diseases of the blood itself may involve the red blood cells, white blood cells, or platelets or the tissues in which these elements are formed—the bone marrow, lymph nodes, and spleen—or of bleeding and blood clotting. Certain features of physical examination are especially important in the diagnosis of disease, including those of the blood. Particularly in the case of blood disorders, important physiological changes may include the presence or absence of pallor or, the opposite, an excess of colour; jaundice, red tongue, and enlargement of the heart, liver, spleen, or lymph nodes; small purple spots or larger bruises on the skin; and tenderness of the bones.

LABORATORY EXAMINATION OF BLOOD

Physicians rely on laboratory analysis to obtain measurements of many constituents of the blood, information useful or necessary for the detection and recognition of disease. One such constituent is hemoglobin, which contains a highly coloured pigment that interferes with the passage of a beam of light. To measure hemoglobin concentration, blood is diluted and the red blood cells broken down to yield a clear red solution. A photoelectric instrument is used to measure the absorbance of transmitted light, from which hemoglobin concentration can be calculated.

Changes in the hemoglobin concentration of the blood are not necessarily directly paralleled by changes in the red cell count and the hematocrit value, because the size and hemoglobin concentration of red cells may change in disease. Therefore, measurements of the red cell count and the hematocrit value may provide useful information as well. Electronic particle counters for determining red cell, white cell, and platelet counts are widely used. Only a drop of blood is needed for the analyses, which are completed within a minute.

Adequate examination of the blood cells requires that a thin film of blood be spread on a glass slide, stained with

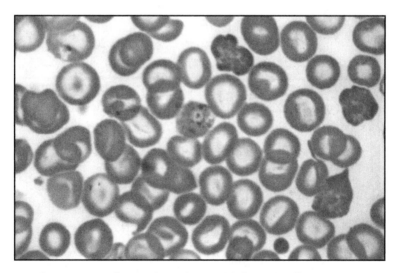

Wright staining is frequently used to highlight and differentiate between blood cells. The microscopic examination of stained cells aids in the detection of blood abnormalities and diseases. CDC/Steven Glenn/Laboratory & Consultation Division

a special blood stain (Wright stain), and examined under the microscope. Individual red cells, white cells, and platelets are examined, and the relative proportions of the several classes of white cells are tabulated. The results may have important diagnostic implications. In iron deficiency anemia, for example, the red cells look paler than normal because they lack the normal amount of hemoglobin. In malaria the diagnosis is established by observing the malarial parasites within the red cells. In pneumonia and many infections, the proportion of neutrophilic white cells is usually increased, whereas in others, such as pertussis (whooping cough) and measles, there is an increase in the proportion of lymphocytes.

Chemical analyses measure many of the constituents of plasma. Often serum rather than plasma is used, however, because serum can be obtained from clotted blood without the addition of an anticoagulant. Changes in the concentrations of chemical constituents of the blood can indicate the presence of disease. For example, quantitative determination of the amount of sugar (glucose) in the blood is essential for the diagnosis of diabetes, a disease in which the blood sugar tends to be elevated. Nitrogenous waste products, in particular urea, tend to accumulate in persons with diseased kidneys that are unable to excrete these substances at a normal rate. An increased concentration of bilirubin in the serum often reflects a disorder of the liver and bile ducts or an increased rate of destruction of hemoglobin.

Although tests can be performed manually using an individual procedure for each analysis, the autoanalyzer, a completely automated machine, increases the number of chemical analyses that can be performed in laboratories. A dozen analyses may be made simultaneously by a single machine employing a small amount of serum. The serum is automatically drawn from a test tube and propelled through plastic tubing of small diameter. As the serum specimen advances, it is divided and appropriate reagents are added. Chemical reactions occur with formation of a product that can be measured with a photoelectric instrument, and the result appears as a written tracing from which serum concentration of various substances can be read directly. The data acquired by the machine may be fed automatically into a computer and the numerical results printed on a form that is submitted to a physician. Many available analyses are not routinely performed but are invaluable in special circumstances. In cases of suspected lead poisoning, for example, detection of an elevated lead level in the blood may be diagnostic. Some analytical procedures have specific diagnostic usefulness such as assays for certain hormones, which include measurement of the thyroid hormone in the serum of patients suspected of having thyroid disease.

Other important laboratory procedures are concerned with immunologic reactions of the blood. Careful determinations of the blood groups of the patient and the blood donor, and crossmatching of the cells of one with the serum of the other to ensure compatibility, are essential for the safe transfusion of blood. The Rh type of a pregnant woman is regularly determined and is necessary for the early detection of fetal-maternal incompatibility and for proper prevention or treatment of erythroblastosis fetalis. The diagnosis of certain infectious diseases depends on the demonstration of antibodies in the patient's serum.

Many other kinds of blood examination yield useful results. Enzymes normally present in the muscle of the heart may be released into the blood when the heart is damaged by a coronary occlusion (obstruction of the coronary artery) with consequent tissue death. Measurement of these enzymes in the serum is regularly performed to assist in diagnosis of this type of heart disease. Damage to the liver releases other enzymes, measurement of which aids in evaluation of the nature and severity of liver disease. Inherited abnormalities of proteins are increasingly recognized and identified by use of sophisticated methods. Accurate diagnosis of hemophilia and other bleeding disorders is made possible by investigations of the coagulation mechanism. Measurements of the concentration of folic acid and vitamin B_{12} in the blood provide the basis for diagnosis of deficiencies of these vitamins.

BLOOD ANALYSIS

Blood analysis is used to obtain information about the physical and chemical properties of blood and is commonly carried out on a blood sample drawn from the vein of the arm, finger, or earlobe. In some cases, the blood cells of the bone marrow may also be examined. Hundreds of hematological tests and procedures have been developed, and many can be carried out simultaneously on one sample of blood with such instruments as autoanalyzers.

SERUM AND SERUM ALBUMIN

Biochemical testing of serum and plasma is an important part of modern clinical diagnosis and treatment monitoring. High or low concentrations of glucose in the plasma or serum help confirm serious disorders such as diabetes mellitus and hypoglycemia. Serum and the protein serum albumin in particular can be readily prepared and analyzed for diagnostic purposes. Serum is the portion of plasma remaining after coagulation of blood, a process during which plasma protein fibrinogen is converted to fibrin and remains behind in the clot. Antiserum, which is prepared from the blood of animals or humans that have been exposed to a disease and have developed specific antibodies, is used to protect persons against disease to which they have been exposed.

Serum albumin, which is a protein occurring in abundance in the plasma, helps maintain the osmotic pressure between the blood vessels and tissues. Serum albumin accounts for 55 percent of the total protein in blood plasma. Circulating blood tends to force fluid out of the blood vessels and into the tissues, where it results in edema (swelling from excess fluid). The colloid nature of albumin—and, to a lesser extent, of other blood proteins called globulins—keeps the fluid within the blood vessels. Albumin also acts as a carrier for two materials necessary for the control of blood clotting: (1) antithrombin, which keeps the clotting enzyme thrombin from working unless needed, and (2) heparin cofactor, which is necessary for the anticlotting action of heparin. The serum albumin level falls and rises in such liver disorders as cirrhosis or hepatitis. Transfusions of serum albumin are used to combat shock and whenever it is necessary to remove excess fluid from the tissues. Similar albumin compounds with other functions occur in plants, animal tissues, egg whites, and milk.

PLASMA

In the laboratory, plasma is derived when all the blood cells—red blood cells, white blood cells, and platelets—are separated from whole blood. The remaining straw-coloured fluid is 90–92 percent water, but it contains critical solutes necessary for sustaining health and life. Important constituents include electrolytes such as sodium, potassium, chloride, bicarbonate, magnesium, and calcium. In addition, there are trace amounts of other substances, including amino acids, vitamins, organic acids, pigments, and enzymes. Hormones such as insulin, corticosteroids, and thyroxine are secreted into the blood by the endocrine system. Plasma concentrations of hormones must be carefully regulated for good health. Nitrogenous wastes (e.g., urea and creatinine) transported to the kidney for excretion increase markedly with renal failure.

The electrolytes and acid-base system found in the plasma are finely regulated. For example, potassium is normally present in plasma in a concentration of only 4 milliequivalents per litre. A slight rise in plasma potassium (to 6–7 milliequivalents per litre) can result in death. Likewise, sodium, chloride, bicarbonate, calcium, and magnesium levels in the plasma must be precisely maintained within a narrow range. Smaller molecules such as sodium, potassium, glucose, and calcium are primarily responsible for the concentration of dissolved particles in the plasma. However, the concentration of much larger proteins (especially albumin) on either side of semipermeable membranes, such as the endothelial cells lining the capillaries, creates crucial pressure gradients necessary to maintain the correct amount of water within the intravascular compartment and, therefore, to regulate the volume of circulating blood. So, for example, patients who have kidney dysfunction or low plasma protein concentrations (especially low albumin) may develop a migration of water from the vascular space into the tissue spaces, causing edema (swelling) and congestion in the extremities and vital organs, including the lungs.

In contrast, substances produced as a consequence of disease may be secreted from cells and tissues into the plasma. Certain substances released into the plasma by cancers may indicate an occult malignancy. For instance, an increased concentration of prostate-specific antigen (PSA) in a middle-aged asymptomatic man may indicate undiagnosed prostate cancer.

Separation of Plasma and Serum

Blood is composed of plasma and blood cells, which are suspended in the plasma with other particulate matter. Plasma is a clear straw-coloured fluid that makes up more than half the volume of blood. It is distinguished from serum, the clear cell-free fluid in which fibrinogen, a soluble protein normally found in the plasma, has been converted to fibrin, an insoluble clotting protein, and from which fibrin and other clotting proteins have been removed. Serum is formed when the plasma or whole blood is allowed to clot. Centrifugation can be used to separate the plasma or serum from blood samples. Tests to measure the concentration of substances in the blood may use plasma, serum, or whole blood that has been anticoagulated to keep all the contents in suspension.

Measurable Properties of Blood

Many tests are designed to determine the number of red and white cells in the blood, together with the volume, sedimentation rate, and hemoglobin concentration of the red blood cells (blood count). In addition, certain tests are used to classify blood according to specific red blood cell antigens, or blood groups. Other tests elucidate the shape and structural details of blood cells and hemoglobin and other blood proteins. Blood also can be analyzed to determine the activity of various enzymes, or protein catalysts, that either are associated with the blood cells or found free in the blood plasma.

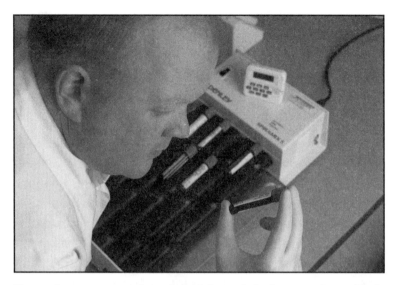

Type, volume, enzyme and protein activity, and clotting rate, along with the presence of infection, can all be determined by testing a small blood sample in a laboratory. Taxi/Getty Images

Blood also may be analyzed on the basis of properties such as total volume, circulation time, viscosity, clotting time and clotting abnormalities, acidity (pH), levels of oxygen and carbon dioxide, and the clearance rate of various substances. There are also special tests based on the presence in the blood of substances characteristic of specific infections, such as the serological tests for syphilis, hepatitis, and human immunodeficiency virus (HIV; the virus that causes AIDS).

BLOOD CELL COUNT

A complete blood count (CBC) is a measure of the hematologic parameters of the blood. Included in the CBC is the calculation of the number of red blood cells (red blood cell count) or white blood cells (white blood cell count) in a cubic millimetre (mm^3) of blood, a differential white blood cell count, a hemoglobin assay, a hematocrit, calculations of red cell volume, and a platelet count. (See pp. 228 for hematology reference values.) The differential white blood cell count includes measurements of the different types of white blood cells that constitute the total white blood cell count: the band neutrophils, segmented neutrophils, lymphocytes, monocytes, eosinophils, and basophils. A specific infection can be suspected on the basis of the type of white cell that has an abnormal value. Viral infections usually affect the lymphocyte count, whereas bacterial infections increase the percentage of band neutrophils. Eosinophils are increased in patients with allergic conditions and some parasitic infections. The immune system of a healthy individual responds to infection by increasing the number of white blood cells. However, the immune system infected with HIV, which damages the body's ability to fight infection, is unable to mount a defense of white blood cells (namely, lymphocytes) and cannot defend the body against viral, bacterial, or parasitic assault.

Calculations of red blood cells provide important information on the possible etiology (origin) of a disease. For example, the mean corpuscular volume (MCV) is the most useful indicator for anemia. The reticulocyte count, which measures the number of young red blood cells being produced, is used to distinguish between anemias resulting from a decrease in production of red cells and those caused by an increase in destruction or loss of red cells. An increase in the number of red blood cells (polycythemia) is normal for persons living at high altitudes, but in most of the population it indicates disease.

Platelets, small structures that are 2 to 4 micrometres in diameter, play a role in blood clotting. A decrease in the platelet count can result in bleeding if the number falls to a value less than 20,000 platelets per microlitre. Counts greater than 50,000 to 100,000 per microlitre may be required for invasive or surgical procedures. Platelet function is important. For example, patients with a normal platelet count and who have been on anticoagulant drugs such as aspirin may have increased or severe bleeding when subjected to cardiovascular surgical procedures.

Hematopoiesis (the production of blood cells) occurs in the bone marrow, and many types of blood disorders can be best diagnosed by analyzing a sample of bone marrow removed by a needle from the centre of the pelvic bone or the sternum (bone marrow biopsy).

COAGULATION TESTS

Bleeding disorders are suspected when blood is seen in the skin (purpura) or when a wound is delayed in clotting. In addition to a low platelet count in the peripheral blood, there may be a decrease in megakaryocytes, cells in the bone marrow that form platelets. A bleeding time longer than 20 minutes indicates abnormal platelet function. Other screening tests for coagulation disorders include the prothrombin time (PT) test, the activated partial thromboplastin time (APTT) test, and the plasma fibrinogen assay. Specific procoagulant proteins, which are enzymes essential to the clotting of blood, should be assayed if a disorder associated with one of them is suspected. For example, factors VIII or IX can be assayed if the patient is thought to have hemophilia A or B, respectively. Deep-seated hemorrhages into joints or tissue spaces after apparent minor trauma and a family history of bleeding disorders may indicate hereditary hemophilia.

SEDIMENTATION AND COMPATIBILITY TESTS

The erythrocyte sedimentation rate (ESR) is the rate at which red blood cells settle in a column of blood in one hour. It is a nonspecific indicator of inflammatory disease that is also increased in anemia. When blood cells clump together, owing to the presence of inflammatory factors or coagulation proteins such as fibrinogen, red cells fall more rapidly out of solution than they do when they do not adhere to one another. The faster cells fall out of the solution, the higher the sedimentation rate.

The Coombs, or antiglobulin, test (AGT) is used to test red blood cells for compatibility when doing a cross-match between donor red blood cells and recipient serum. The AGT test detects antibodies that would cause life-threatening immune destruction during the transfusion of red blood cells. It also is used to detect antibodies to red blood cells in hemolytic disease in newborns and drug-induced hemolytic anemias.

HEMATOCRIT

The hematocrit is a diagnostic procedure that is used for the analysis of blood. The name is also used for the apparatus in which this procedure is performed and for the results of the analysis. In the procedure, an anticoagulant is added to a blood sample held in a calibrated tube. The tube is allowed to stand for one hour, after which the sedimentation rate (how rapidly blood cells settle out from plasma) is determined. Most acute generalized infections and some local infections raise the rate of sedimentation. A raised sedimentation rate may be among the first signs of an otherwise hidden disease.

In the second phase of the procedure, the tube is centrifuged so that its contents separate into three layers—packed red blood cells at the bottom, a reddish gray layer of white blood cells and platelets in the middle, and plasma at the top. The hematocrit is expressed as the percentage of the total blood volume occupied by the packed red blood cells. The depths of these layers are indicative of health or disease. The red blood cell layer is abnormally thick in the disease polycythemia and too thin in iron-deficiency anemia. White blood cells are too abundant in leukemia. Finally, plasma is deep yellow in jaundice (often caused by liver disease). The hematocrit is among the most commonly used of all laboratory diagnostic procedures.

SEROLOGICAL TESTS

Serological tests are any of several laboratory procedures carried out on a sample of blood serum. The purpose of such a test is to detect serum antibodies or antibody-like substances that appear specifically in association with certain diseases. The most common complement-fixation tests are flocculation tests. They are based on the precipitation, or flocculation, that takes place when the antibody and specially prepared antigens are mixed together. Neutralization tests depend on the capacity of the antibody to neutralize the infectious properties of the infectious organisms. Finally, hemagglutinin-inhibition tests make use of the finding that certain viruses will cause the red blood cells of certain animal species to agglutinate (congeal, or clump together) and that this agglutination will be prevented by the antibody.

Serological testing is particularly helpful in the diagnosis of rickettsial and viral diseases such as Rocky Mountain spotted fever, influenza, measles, poliomyelitis, and yellow fever, as well as of infectious mononucleosis and rheumatoid arthritis. As a practical mass-screening diagnostic tool, it has proved valuable in the detection of conditions such as syphilis.

METHODS OF BLOOD GROUPING

There are several approaches to the identification of blood groups on red cells. Included among these are tests for various types of antibody–antigen reactions and methods for the separation of individual antibodies that can then be investigated and described. In some cases, more than one test is used for accurate blood group identification and characterization.

IDENTIFICATION OF BLOOD GROUPS

The basic technique in identification of the antigens and antibodies of blood groups is the agglutination test. Agglutination of red cells results from antibody cross-linkages established when different specific combining sites of one antibody react with antigen on two different red cells. By mixing red cells (antigen) and serum (antibody), either the type of antigen or the type of antibody can be determined depending on whether a cell of known antigen composition or a serum with known antibody specificity is used.

In its simplest form, a volume of serum containing antibody is added to a thin suspension (2–5 percent) of red cells suspended in physiological saline solution in a small tube with a narrow diameter. After incubation at the appropriate temperature, the red cells will have settled to the bottom of the tube. These sedimented red cells are examined macroscopically (with the naked eye) for agglutination, or they may be spread on a slide and viewed through a low-power microscope.

An antibody that agglutinates red cells when they are suspended in saline solution is called a complete antibody. With powerful complete antibodies, such as anti-A and anti-B, agglutination reactions visible to the naked eye take place when a drop of antibody is placed on a slide together with a drop containing red cells in suspension. After stirring, the slide is rocked, and agglutination is visible in a few minutes. It is always necessary in blood grouping to include a positive and a negative control for each test.

An antibody that does not clump red cells when they are suspended in saline solution is called incomplete. Such antibodies block the antigenic sites of the red cells so that subsequent addition of complete antibody of the same antigenic specificity does not result in agglutination. Incomplete antibodies will agglutinate red cells carrying the appropriate antigen, however, when the cells are suspended in media containing protein. Serum albumin from the blood of cattle is frequently used for this purpose. Red cells may also be rendered specifically agglutinable by incomplete antibodies after treatment with such protease enzymes as trypsin, papain, ficin, or bromelain.

After infections such as pneumonia, red cells may become agglutinable by almost all normal sera because of exposure of a hidden antigenic site (T) as a result of the action of bacterial enzymes. When the patient recovers, the blood also returns to normal with respect to agglutination. It is unusual for the red cells to reflect antigenicity other than that determined by the individual's genetic makeup. The presence of an acquired B antigen on the red cells has been described occasionally in diseases of the colon, thus allowing the red cell to express an antigenicity other than that genetically determined. Other diseases may alter immunoglobulins. For example, some may induce the production of antibodies directed against the person's own blood groups (autoimmune hemolytic anemia) and thus may interfere with blood grouping. In other diseases, a defect in antibody synthesis may cause the absence of anti-A and anti-B antibody.

Coombs Test

When an incomplete antibody reacts with the red cells in saline solution, the antigenic sites become coated with antibody globulin (gamma globulin), and no visible agglutination reaction takes place. The presence of gamma globulin on cells can be detected by the Coombs test, named for its inventor, English immunologist Robert Coombs. Coombs serum (also called antihuman globulin) is made by immunizing rabbits with human gamma globulin. The rabbits respond by making antihuman globulin (i.e., antibodies against human gamma globulin and complement) that is then purified before use. The antihuman globulin usually contains antibodies against IgG and

Centrifuging a specially prepared blood sample is the final step of a Coombs test, used to determine the presence of certain antibodies on cells that may indicate disease or type incompatibility. Dana Neely/Taxi/Getty Images

complement. Coombs serum is added to the washed cells and the tube is centrifuged. Finally, if the cells are coated by gamma globulin or complement, agglutinates will form. Newer antiglobulin reagents (made by immunizing with purified protein) can detect either globulin or complement. Depending on how it is performed, the Coombs test can detect incomplete antibody in the serum or antibody bound to the red cell membrane. In certain diseases, anemia may be caused when gamma globulin coats red cells. This can happen when a mother has made antibodies against the red cells of her newborn child or if a person makes an autoantibody against his or her own red cells.

ADSORPTION, ELUTION, AND TITRATION

If a serum sample contains a mixture of antibodies, it is possible to prepare pure samples of each by a technique called adsorption. In this technique an unwanted antibody is removed by mixing it with red cells carrying the appropriate antigen. The antigen interacts with the antibody and binds it to the cell surface. These red cells are washed thoroughly and spun down tightly by centrifugation. When all the fluid above the cells is removed, the cells are said to be packed. The cells are packed to avoid dilution of the antibody being prepared. Adsorption, then, is a method of separating mixtures of antibodies by removing some and leaving others. It is used to identify antibody mixtures and to purify reagents. The purification of the Coombs serum is done in the same way.

If red cells have adsorbed gamma globulin onto their surfaces, the antibody can sometimes be recovered by a process known as elution. One simple way of eluting (dissociating) antibody from washed red cells is to heat them at 56 °C (133 °F) in a small volume of saline solution. Other methods include use of acid or ether. This technique is sometimes useful in the identification of antibodies.

Titration is used to determine the strength of an antibody. Doubling dilutions of the antibody are made in a suitable medium in a series of tubes. Cells carrying the appropriate antigen are added, and the agglutination reactions are read and scored for the degree of positivity. The actual concentration of the antibody is given by the dilution at which some degree of agglutination, however weak, can still be seen. This would be an unsafe dilution to use for blood-grouping purposes. If an antiserum can be diluted, the dilution chosen must be such that strong positive reactions occur with selected positive control cells. Titration is helpful when preparing reagents and comparing antibody concentrations at different time intervals.

Inhibition Tests

Inhibition tests are used to detect the presence of antigen with blood group specificity in solutions. Inhibition of a known antibody–antigen reaction by a fluid indicates a particular blood group specificity. If an active substance is added to an antibody, neutralization of the antibody's activity prevents agglutination when red cells carrying the appropriate antigen are subsequently added to the mixture. A, B, Lewis, Chido, Rogers, and P antigens are readily available and can be used to facilitate antibody identification. This technique was used to elucidate the biochemistry of ABH, Ii, and Lewis systems, and it is important in forensic medicine as a means of identifying antigens in blood stains.

HEMOLYSIS

Laboratory tests in which hemolysis (destruction) of the red cells is the end point are infrequently used in blood grouping. For hemolysis to take place, a particular component of fresh serum called complement must be present. Complement must be added to the mixture of antibody and red cells. It may sometimes be desirable to look for hemolysins that destroy group A red cells in mothers whose group A children are incompatible or in individuals, not belonging to groups A or AB, who have been immunized with tetanus toxoid that contains substances with group A specificity.

Hemolytic reactions may occur in patients who have been given transfusions of blood that either is incompatible or has already hemolyzed. The sera of such patients require special investigations to detect the presence of hemoglobin that has escaped from red cells destroyed within the body and for the breakdown products of other red cell constituents.

SOURCES OF ANTIBODIES AND ANTIGENS

Normal donors are used as the source of supply of naturally occurring antibodies, such as those of the ABO, P, and Lewis systems. Because these antibodies work best at temperatures below that of the body (37 °C [98.6 °F]), in the case of what are known as cold agglutinins (such as anti-P_I), the antibody is most active at 4 °C (39 °F). Most antibodies used in blood grouping must be searched for in immunized donors.

Antibodies for MN typing are usually raised in rabbits — similarly for the Coombs serum. Antibodies prepared in this way must be absorbed free of unwanted components and carefully standardized before use. Additional substances with specific blood group activity have been found in certain plants. Plant agglutinins are called lectins. Some useful reagents extracted from seeds are anti-H from *Ulex europaeus* (common gorse); anti-A$_1$, from another member of the pulse family Fabaceae (Leguminosae), *Dolichos biflorus*; and anti-N from the South American plant *Vicia graminea*. Agglutinins have also been found in animals—for example, the fluid pressed from the land snail *Octala lactea*. Additional plant lectins and agglutinins from animal fluids have been isolated.

Monoclonal antibodies (structurally identical antibodies produced by hybridomas) to blood groups are replacing some of the human blood grouping reagents. Mouse hybridomas (hybrid cells of a myeloma tumour cell and lymphocyte merging) produce anti-A and anti-B monoclonal antibodies. The antibodies are made by immunizing with either red cells or synthetic carbohydrates. In addition to their use in blood grouping, these monoclonal antibodies can help define the hereditary background (heterogenicity) and structure of the red cell antigen.

Blood Bank

An organization that collects, stores, processes, and transfuses blood is known as a blood bank. During World War I it was demonstrated that stored blood could safely be used, allowing for the development of the first blood bank in 1932. Before the first blood banks came into operation, a physician determined the blood types of the patient's relatives and friends until the proper type was found, performed the crossmatch, bled the donor, and gave the transfusion to the patient. In the 1940s the discovery of many blood types and several crossmatching techniques led to the rapid development of blood banking as a specialized field and a gradual shift of responsibility for the technical

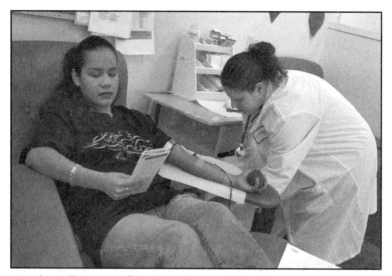

As only small amounts of blood are taken during blood donation, the procedure has a negligible effect on the donor. Tim Boyle/Getty Images

aspects of transfusion from practicing physicians to technicians and clinical pathologists. The practicality of storing fresh blood and blood components for future needs made possible such innovations as artificial kidneys, heart-lung pumps for open-heart surgery, and exchange transfusions for infants with erythroblastosis fetalis.

Whole blood is donated and stored in units of about 450 ml (slightly less than 1 pint). Whole blood can be stored only for a limited time, but various components (e.g., red blood cells and plasma) can be frozen and stored for a year or longer. Therefore, most blood donations are separated and stored as components by the blood bank. These components include platelets to control bleeding; concentrated red blood cells to correct anemia; and plasma fractions, such as fibrinogen to aid clotting, immune globulins to prevent and treat a number of infectious diseases, and serum albumin to augment the blood volume in cases of shock. Thus, it is possible to serve the varying needs of five or more patients with a single blood donation.

Despite such replacement programs, many blood banks face continual problems in obtaining sufficient donations. The chronic shortage of donors has been alleviated somewhat by the development of apheresis, a technique by which only a desired blood component is taken from the donor's blood, with the remaining fluid and blood cells immediately transfused back into the donor. This technique allows the collection of large amounts of a particular component, such as platelets, from a single donor.

THERAPEUTIC APPLICATIONS

The therapeutic applications of blood and blood analyses fill an important niche in medicine. The transfusion of blood from a healthy person into a person affected by disease or trauma is a lifesaving procedure. Likewise, the development of highly sensitive blood tests and improved blood collection techniques has significantly advanced organ and bone marrow transplants, thereby providing therapeutic approaches for several historically untreatable and potentially fatal conditions.

BLOOD TRANSFUSION

The transfer of blood into the vein of a human or animal recipient characterizes the process of blood transfusion. The transfused blood either is taken directly from a donor or obtained from a blood bank. Blood transfusions are a therapeutic measure used to restore blood or plasma volume after extensive hemorrhage, burns, or trauma; increase the number and concentration of red blood cells in persons with anemia to improve the oxygen-carrying capacity of their blood; and treat shock. Transfusions are a crucial adjunct in some types of surgery in which patients lose large amounts of whole blood that must be replaced.

Transfusion Procedures and Blood Storage

The procedure for transfusing blood is simple and straightforward. About 450 ml (1 pint) or more of blood is withdrawn from a donor's arm vein by means of a hypodermic syringe and is passed through a plastic tube to a collection bag or bottle to which sodium citrate has been added to prevent the blood from clotting. In transfusing blood into the recipient, donor blood of the appropriate type is passed by gravity from a container down through a plastic tube and into a vein of the recipient's arm. The procedure is accomplished slowly, and two hours may be needed to infuse 450 ml of blood into the recipient. The use of sterile containers, tubing, and needles helps ensure that transfused or stored blood is not exposed to disease-causing microorganisms. Blood can be kept in a state satisfactory for use in transfusion by the addition of special preservatives and refrigeration. Methods of fractionating the blood have allowed its use in specialized forms:

- Whole blood, which is used to treat acute blood loss.
- Packed red blood cells, which are used for chronic anemia.
- Washed red cells, to combat allergies that have been induced in frequently transfused patients by other elements in the blood.
- Platelets, for bleeding caused by platelet deficiency.
- White blood cells, for low white-cell count in patients with infections.
- Plasma, for shock without blood loss.

- Fresh-frozen plasma, freshly drawn plasma, or concentrates of the antihemophilic globulin (factor VIII) of plasma, for bleeding in hemophilia.
- Serum albumin, concentrated from the plasma, for shock or chronic low-albumin disorders and malnutrition.
- Immune globulin, the antibody component of the plasma, concentrated for prevention of viral hepatitis and protection against or modification of measles after exposure.
- Fibrinogen, an important clotting factor in the blood, easily concentrated for bleeding conditions caused by deficiency or absence of fibrinogen.

Exchange transfusion, in which all or most of the patient's blood is removed while new blood is simultaneously transfused, helps treat erythroblastosis fetalis and leukemia and remove certain poisons from the body.

Developments in Transfusion Therapy

The first documented records of intravenous blood transfusions date from Europe about the mid-17th century, but so many patients died from the resulting incompatibility reactions that the process was banned in France, England, and Italy late in the century. Transfusion, which today is a frequent and lifesaving procedure, did not become useful or safe until the blood group antigens and antibodies were discovered. The first system to be identified was the ABO blood group system in 1901. In 1940 the second major system—the Rh (Rhesus) blood group system—was identified. Thereafter, the routine blood typing of donors

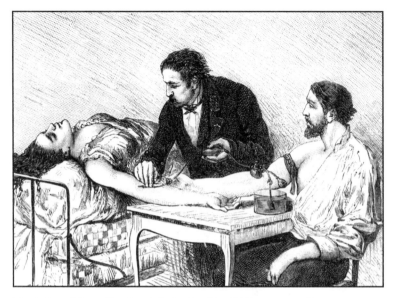

Depiction of direct blood transfusion in 1882. © Photos.com/Jupiterimages

and recipients permitted successful transfusions of blood between them.

In the 1970s, it was discovered that blood transfusions presented a significant risk for the transmission of life-threatening viruses. During the 1970s and early 1980s, testing donors for infectious markers of hepatitis B virus (HBV), such as hepatitis B surface antigen (HBsAg) and an antibody to the so-called core antigen (anti-HBc), greatly reduced the risk of HBV transmission. Shortly thereafter another transfusion-transmitted virus, called hepatitis C virus (HCV), was identified as the principal agent of what was then known as non-A, non-B hepatitis. People infected with HCV produce an antibody called anti-HCV, which can be detected in screening tests. Since 1998 it has been possible to screen for the presence of HCV nucleic acids using polymerase chain reaction (PCR) technology. This molecular detection system can identify HCV in donors before they have produced antibodies, and its use in effective screening programs has greatly reduced the risk of transfusion-transmitted HCV.

Similar progress has been made in testing donors for evidence of human immunodeficiency virus (HIV). In the early 1980s, when it was realized that HIV, which gives rise to acquired immunodeficiency syndrome (AIDS), could be transmitted via blood transfusion, concern about the safety of transfusion increased significantly. Today, however, all blood donors are tested for antibodies to HIV, for an important HIV core antigen called p24, and for HIV nucleic acids. These tests, along with appropriate questioning and screening of donors, have substantially reduced the risk of HIV infection through blood transfusion.

In the 1980s other viruses were also discovered in blood used for transfusions. For example, cytomegalovirus (CMV), a large deoxyribonucleic acid (DNA) virus, is harboured within white blood cells in about 50 to 60 percent of healthy blood donors. In general, CMV is not a threat to transfusion recipients unless their immune systems are suppressed. The risk of CMV transmission has been dramatically reduced by screening donors for the antibody to CMV, as well as by leukoreduction using special filters to remove white cells from blood components. Two other viruses—human T-cell lymphotropic viruses I and II (HTLV-I and HTLV-II), which are in the same family of retroviruses as HIV—are similar to CMV in that they appear to be strictly associated with white cells. Tests developed in the late 1980s enabled screening for serum antibodies to HTLV-I/II and, along with leukoreduction, have greatly reduced the risk of HTLV-I/II transmission.

In addition to the risk of viral transmission, other infectious agents may be transfusion transmitted. For example, there is some risk of bacterial contamination in blood components. This is especially true of platelet components, which are stored at room temperature. Bacterial contamination, although extremely rare, can cause fever, shock, and death if not recognized and treated early. The use of solvents and detergents to treat plasma has virtually eliminated the risk of HBV, HCV, HIV, and HTLV-I/II transmission via transfusion. This solvent detergent treatment process, which is approved and licensed by the U.S. Food and Drug Administration (FDA), has been made readily available to blood centres. Solvent detergent treatment does not work for all blood components, however, including whole blood, red blood cells, and platelet concentrates, because this treatment can destroy vital cellular constituents. Scientists are working to develop safe additives capable of neutralizing or killing viruses and bacteria.

Shortages in blood supplies and concerns about the safety of donated blood have fueled the development of so-called blood substitutes. The two major types of blood substitutes are volume expanders, which include solutions such as saline that are used to replace lost plasma volume, and oxygen therapeutics, agents designed to replace oxygen normally carried by hemoglobin in red blood cells. Of these two types of blood substitutes, the development of oxygen therapeutics has been the most challenging. One of the first groups of agents developed and tested were perfluorocarbons, which effectively transport and deliver oxygen to tissues but cause complex side effects, including flulike reactions, and are not metabolized by the body. Today some of the most promising oxygen therapeutics are agents called hemoglobin-based oxygen carriers (HBOCs), which are made by genetically or chemically engineering hemoglobin isolated from the red blood cells of humans or bovines. HBOCs do not require refrigeration, are compatible with all blood types, and efficiently distribute oxygen to tissues. However, HBOCs and other synthetic oxygen-carrying products have not been approved for use in humans. A primary concern associated with these agents is their potential to cause severe immune reactions.

Transfusion-induced Immune Reactions

Undesirable reactions to transfusion are common and may occur for many reasons, such as allergy, sensitivity to donor white cells, or undetected red cell incompatibility. Unexplained reactions are also fairly common. Rare causes of transfusion reaction include contaminated blood, air bubbles in the blood, overloading of the circulatory system through administration of excess blood, or sensitivity to donor plasma or platelets.

One type of immunologic transfusion reaction is incompatibility in ABO blood groups, which can cause a rapid immune response within blood vessels. This response, known as an intravascular hemolytic reaction, can potentially result in death and is sometimes caused by misidentification of patients, misidentification of blood samples, or mislabeling of blood components. Other, less severe immunologic reactions include hives, or urticarial reactions, caused by sensitization to plasma proteins. These reactions are easily treated by the use of antihistamines prior to the transfusion. In rare cases, a patient may make antibodies to immunoglobulin A (IgA) found in plasma, platelets, whole blood, and packed red blood cells of all donors. Described as IgA-deficient because they do not make IgA, these patients can have a severe allergic reaction characterized by anaphylaxis with vascular collapse, severe drop in blood pressure, and respiratory distress. This problem can be treated by using washed red cells to remove the remaining plasma containing IgA or by using blood components from IgA-negative donors. Patients who receive multiple transfusions may develop antibodies to white cells and experience a brisk febrile reaction following transfusion. This can be prevented by using leukoreduced blood components. Transfusions can also stimulate the production of antibodies to platelets, causing affected patients to be refractory to future platelet transfusions.

Transfusion-related acute lung injury (TRALI) can occur as a complication of transfusion therapy. It can cause severe pulmonary edema and is a life-threatening complication if the patient is not given immediate respiratory support. Although the etiology of TRALI remains unclear, it may result from white cell antibodies in donor blood that attack the white cells of the recipient. Immune-compromised individuals receiving blood transfusions may develop graft-versus-host disease (GVHD), which is caused by the transfusion of donor lymphocytes into the recipient. The immune systems of these recipients are unable to eliminate the lymphocytes. When the transfused lymphocytes proliferate, they can attack the patient's liver, skin, and gastrointestinal tract, leading to GVHD. This disease can be prevented by irradiation of all blood components with at least 3,000 rads (units of radiation) of X-rays, which prevent the transfused white cells from reproducing. Blood components can also cause nonspecific immune suppression of the recipient. The mechanism for this is unknown, but many studies have claimed that transfusion therapy can reduce a recipient's resistance to cancer and infection, especially bacterial infection. Complications from immune suppression can be prevented by reducing unnecessary blood transfusions and by using autologous (self) blood components when appropriate.

ORGAN TRANSPLANT

Organ transplantation involves the removal of a section of tissue or a complete organ from its original natural site and the transfer of that tissue or organ to a new position in the same person or a separate individual. The term, like the synonym graft, was borrowed by surgeons from horticulture. Both words imply that success will result in a healthy and flourishing graft or transplant, which will gain its nourishment from its new environment.

Immune reactions that lead to transplant rejection are the greatest problem in successful tissue and organ grafting. The factors that provoke graft rejection are called transplantation, or histocompatibility, antigens. If donor and recipient have the same antigens, as do identical twins, there can be no rejection. All cells in the body have transplantation antigens except the red blood cells, which carry their own system of blood-group (ABO) antigens. The main human transplantation antigens—called the major histocompatibility complex, or the HLA (human leukocyte antigens) system—are governed by genes on the sixth chromosome. HLA antigens are divided into two groups: class I antigens, the target of an effector rejection response, and class II antigens, the initiators of the rejection reaction. Unlike class I antigens, class II antigens are not found in all tissues. Certain macrophagelike tissue cells—called dendritic cells because of their fingerlike processes—have a high expression of class II antigens. There has been much interest in trying to remove such cells from an organ graft, so the rejection reaction will not be initiated. There has been some experimental success with this approach, but it has not yet been applied clinically.

Tissue typing involves the identification of an individual's HLA antigens. Lymphocytes are used for typing. It is important also that the red blood cells be grouped, because red cell–group antigens are present in other tissues and can cause graft rejection. Although transplantation antigens are numerous and complicated, the principles of tissue typing are the same as for red cell grouping. The lymphocytes being typed are mixed with a typing reagent, a serum that contains antibodies to certain HLA antigens. If the lymphocytes carry HLA antigens for which the reagent has antibodies, the lymphocytes agglutinate (clump together) or die. Typing serums are obtained from the blood of persons who have rejected grafts or had multiple blood transfusions or multiple pregnancies, because such persons may develop antibodies to transplantation antigens.

If the lymphocytes of both the recipient and the potential donor are killed by a given serum, as far as that typing serum is concerned, the individuals have antigens in common. If neither donor nor recipient lymphocytes are affected, donor and recipient lack common antigens. If the donor lymphocytes are killed but not those of the recipient, an antigen is present in the donor and is missing from the recipient. Thus, by testing their lymphocytes against a spectrum of typing sera, it is possible to determine how closely the recipient and donor match in HLA antigens. As a final precaution before grafting, a direct crossmatch is performed between the recipient's serum and donor lymphocytes. A positive crossmatch usually contraindicates the donor–recipient transplant under consideration.

The aim of transplantation research is to allow the recipient to accept the graft permanently with no unpleasant side effects. With current drugs that are used for this purpose, after some months the dosage can often be reduced and sometimes even stopped without graft rejection. In such a case, the patient is no longer as susceptible to infections. There would appear to be adaptation of the recipient toward the graft and the graft toward the recipient. The adaptation is probably akin to desensitization, a process used sometimes to cure patients suffering from asthma by giving them repeated injections of small doses of the pollen to which they are sensitive.

Paternity Testing

Although blood group studies cannot be used to prove paternity, they can provide unequivocal evidence that a male is not the father of a particular child. Because the red cell antigens are inherited as dominant traits, a child cannot have a blood group antigen that is not present in one or both parents. For example, if the child in question belongs to group A and both the mother and the putative father are group O, the man is excluded from paternity. Furthermore, if one parent is genetically homozygous for a particular antigen—that is, has inherited the gene for it from both the grandfather and grandmother of the child—that antigen must appear in the blood of the child. For example, in the MN system, a father whose phenotype is M and whose genotype is *MM* (in other words, a man who is of blood type M and has inherited the characteristic from both parents) will transmit an *M* allele to all his progeny.

In medicolegal work, it is important that the blood samples are properly identified. By using multiple red cell antigen systems and adding additional studies on other blood types (HLA, red cell enzymes, and plasma proteins), it is possible to state with a high degree of statistical certainty that a particular male is the father.

BONE MARROW AND HEMATOPOIETIC STEM CELLS

A stem cell is an undifferentiated cell that can divide to produce some offspring cells that continue as stem cells and some cells that are destined to differentiate (become specialized). Stem cells are an ongoing source of the differentiated cells that make up the tissues and organs of animals and plants. There is great interest in stem cells because they have potential in the development of therapies for replacing defective or damaged cells resulting from a variety of disorders and injuries, such as Parkinson disease, heart disease, and diabetes.

There are two major types of stem cells: embryonic stem cells and adult stem cells, which are also called tissue stem cells. One of the most important sources of stem cells in humans is bone marrow, but only adult stem cells, which have limited differentiation capabilities relative to embryonic stem cells, can be isolated from bone marrow. Small quantities of adult stem cells also occur in the blood. Because technologies exist for the isolation of stem cells from both bone marrow and blood, these tissues are the subjects of intense scientific research. Much of this research is aimed at the development of new stem cell–based therapies and has led to a tremendous expansion in scientists' knowledge of the molecular biology and behaviour of stem cells.

Bone marrow contains cells called hematopoietic stem cells, which generate all the cell types of the blood and the immune system. Hematopoietic stem cells are also found in small numbers in peripheral blood and in larger numbers in umbilical cord blood. In bone marrow, hematopoietic stem cells are anchored to osteoblasts of the trabecular bone and to blood vessels. They generate progeny that can become lymphocytes, granulocytes, red blood cells, and certain other cell types, depending on the balance of growth factors in their immediate environment.

Work with experimental animals has shown that transplants of hematopoietic stem cells can occasionally colonize other tissues, with the transplanted cells becoming neurons, muscle cells, or epithelia. The degree to which transplanted hematopoietic stem cells are able to colonize other tissues is exceedingly small. Despite this, the use of hematopoietic stem cell transplants is being

Anatomical sources of neural and hematopoietic stem cells

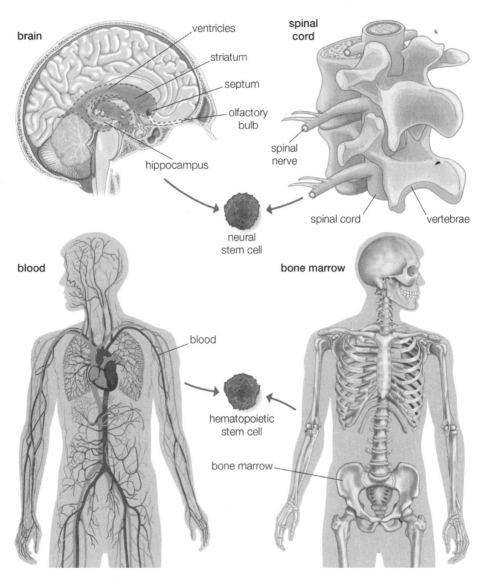

Neural and hematopoietic stem cells have tremendous potential in the development of therapies for certain diseases, such as diabetes and Parkinson disease. Neural stem cells occur in the spinal cord and specific regions of the brain, and hematopoietic stem cells occur in the blood and bone marrow. Encyclopædia Britannica, Inc.

explored for conditions such as heart disease or autoimmune disorders. It is an especially attractive option for those opposed to the use of embryonic stem cells.

Bone marrow transplants (also known as bone marrow grafts) represent a type of stem cell therapy that is in common use. They are used to allow cancer patients to survive otherwise lethal doses of radiation therapy or chemotherapy that destroy the stem cells in bone marrow. For this procedure, the patient's own marrow is harvested before the cancer treatment and is then reinfused into the body after treatment. The hematopoietic stem cells of the transplant colonize the damaged marrow and eventually repopulate the blood and the immune system with functional cells. Bone marrow transplants are also often carried out between individuals (allograft). In this case the grafted marrow has some beneficial antitumour effect. Risks associated with bone marrow allografts include rejection of the graft by the patient's immune system and reaction of immune cells of the graft against the patient's tissues (graft-versus-host disease).

Bone marrow is a source for mesenchymal stem cells (sometimes called marrow stromal cells, or MSCs), which are precursors to non-hematopoietic stem cells that have the potential to differentiate into several distinct types of cells, including cells that form bone, muscle, and connective tissue. In cell cultures, bone marrow–derived mesenchymal stem cells demonstrate pluripotency when exposed to substances that influence cell differentiation. Harnessing these pluripotent properties has become highly valuable in the generation of transplantable tissues and organs. In 2008 scientists used mesenchymal stem cells to bioengineer a section of trachea that was transplanted into a woman whose upper airway had been severely damaged by tuberculosis. The stem cells were derived from the woman's bone marrow, cultured in a laboratory, and used for tissue engineering. In the engineering process, a donor trachea was stripped of its interior and exterior cell linings, leaving behind a trachea "scaffold" of connective tissue. The stem cells derived from the recipient were then used to recolonize the interior of the scaffold, and normal epithelial cells, also isolated from the recipient, were used to recolonize the exterior of the trachea. The use of the recipient's own cells to populate the trachea scaffold prevented immune rejection and eliminated the need for immunosuppression therapy. The transplant, which was successful, was the first of its kind.

BONE MARROW TRANSPLANT

A bone marrow transplant is the transfer of bone marrow from a healthy donor to a recipient whose own bone marrow is affected by disease. Bone marrow transplant may be used to treat aplastic anemia; sickle cell anemia; various malignant diseases of blood-forming tissues, including leukemia, lymphoma, and multiple myeloma; certain solid cancers such as neuroblastoma; immune deficiency diseases; and metabolic diseases.

In 1956 American physician E. Donnall Thomas performed the first successful syngeneic (genetically identical) bone marrow transplant between two humans. The tissues of the recipient, a patient with leukemia, accepted the donated marrow (or graft) from his identical twin and used it to make new, healthy blood cells and immune system cells. Thomas adopted methods to match the tissues of donor and recipient closely enough to minimize the latter's rejection of the former's marrow. He also developed drugs to suppress the immune system, further reducing the chances for graft rejection by the recipient. In 1969 these refinements enabled Thomas to perform the first successful bone marrow transplant in a leukemia patient from a relative who was not an identical twin. In 1990 Thomas was corecipient (with American surgeon Joseph E. Murray) of the Nobel Prize for Physiology or Medicine for his pioneering work on bone marrow transplantation.

AUTOLOGOUS AND ALLOGENEIC TRANSPLANTS

Today, the two most commonly used bone marrow transplants are known as autologous and allogeneic. Both types of transplants are considered forms of stem cell therapy, because hematopoietic stem cells from the bone marrow are central to the recovery of the patient receiving the graft. An autologous transplant is used primarily in the case of cancer patients who are preparing to undergo high

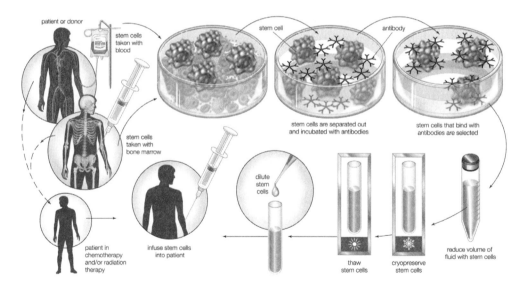

In an autologous bone marrow transplant, hematopoietic stem cells are harvested from the blood or bone marrow of a patient before the patient undergoes treatment for cancer. To remove tumour cells that may have been collected with the stem cells, the sample is incubated with antibodies that bind only to stem cells. The stem cells are then isolated and stored for later use, when they are reinfused into the patient. Encyclopædia Britannica, Inc.

doses of chemotherapy or radiation therapy. Autologous transplant involves harvesting stem cells from the patient's bone marrow and storing these cells prior to therapy. After the patient has undergone therapy to destroy the cancer cells, the stem cells are injected into the bloodstream to speed recovery of the bone marrow.

If an individual's marrow is diseased—from leukemia, for example—a person with a matching tissue type is found to donate stem cells. This type of transplant is called an allogeneic transplant.

Risks of Bone Marrow Transplant

Major risks associated with bone marrow transplant include increased susceptibility to infection, anemia, graft failure, respiratory distress, and excess fluid, which can lead to pneumonia and liver dysfunction. In addition, a mismatch between donor and recipient tissues can lead to an immune reaction between cells of the host and cells of the graft. When graft cells attack host cells, the result is the dangerous condition GVHD, which may be acute or chronic and may manifest as a skin rash, gastrointestinal illness, or liver disease. The risk of GVHD can be minimized through careful tissue-matching. This is done by comparing the cell-surface HLAs, a system of molecules that enable components of the immune system such as T cells to mount an attack against foreign substances. Donor HLA antigens that exactly match those of the recipient increase the chances for a successful transplant. However, even when a donor antigen match is identical, roughly 40 percent of recipients still develop GVHD. This figure increases to between 60 and 80 percent when only a single antigen is mismatched. Because of the danger of this complication, autologous transplants are more commonly performed.

Bone marrow transplantation initially was not recommended for patients older than age 50, because of the higher mortality and morbidity that results and because the incidence of GVHD increases in those older than age 30. However, many transplant centres have performed successful bone marrow transplantations in patients well beyond age 50. People who donate bone marrow incur no risk, because they generate new marrow to replace that which has been removed.

COLLECTION OF DONOR STEM CELLS

Hematopoietic stem cells from a bone marrow donor are collected using apheresis. During this procedure, blood is drawn from one arm and passes through a machine that collects the stem cells. The remaining portion of the blood is then returned to the donor via a catheter inserted in the arm opposite the one from which the blood is drawn. Prior to undergoing apheresis, the donor receives injections of a drug such as filgrastim (granulocyte colony-stimulating factor), which mobilizes stem cells into the peripheral blood circulation. Following donation, some people experience fatigue, nausea, muscle pain, bone pain, and headache. Multiple apheresis sessions may be needed to collect a sufficient number of stem cells from a donor. In rare cases, donors may need to undergo bone marrow harvest. In this procedure, the donor is placed under anesthesia, and bone marrow aspiration is performed, typically taking marrow from the iliac crest of the hip or from the breastbone.

CHAPTER 5

DISEASES OF RED BLOOD CELLS AND HEMOGLOBIN

Diseases of red blood cells and hemoglobin can seriously impair the oxygen-carrying capability of red cells. Lack of oxygen delivery to tissues can lead to tissue hypoxia (low oxygen) or anoxia (absence of oxygen). Without sufficient oxygen, tissues can become severely damaged, to the point where they no longer function properly. If oxygen deprivation is prolonged, tissue death will occur.

A variety of factors can give rise to disorders affecting red blood cells. For example, some conditions are caused by bacterial, parasitic, or viral infection or abnormalities in metabolism. Other conditions may be inherited or may be caused by an acquired genetic mutation. One of the most common diseases that affects red blood cells is anemia, of which there are various types that are differentiated primarily by cause and blood cell morphology.

Hemoglobin diseases are often complex disorders. Important examples of hemoglobin diseases include thalassemia, a deficiency of hemoglobin, and porphyria, a disease characterized by excess production of porphyrins, the pigment-containing components of hemoglobin.

DISORDERS OF RED BLOOD CELLS

The quantity of red blood cells in normal persons varies with age and sex as well as with external conditions, primarily atmospheric pressure. At sea level an average adult male has 5.4 million red cells per cubic millimetre of blood. From the physiological standpoint, it is the quantity of hemoglobin in the blood that is important because this iron-containing protein is required for the transport of oxygen from the lungs to the tissues. Red cells carry an average of 16 grams of hemoglobin per 100 ml of blood. If such blood is centrifuged so that the red cells are packed in a special tube known as the hematocrit, they are found on the average to occupy 47 percent of the volume of the blood. In the average woman, the normal figures are lower than this (red cell count 4.8 million, hemoglobin 14 grams, volume of packed red cells 42 percent). In the newborn infant, these values are higher but decrease in the course of the first several weeks of postnatal life to levels below those of the normal woman. Thereafter they rise gradually. The differences in male and female blood begin to appear at about the time of puberty.

Red cells are formed within the marrow cavities of the central bones of the adult skeleton (skull, spine, ribs, breastbone, pelvic bones). In a healthy person, red cell production (erythropoiesis) is so well adjusted to red cell destruction that the levels of red cells and hemoglobin remain constant. The rate of production of red cells by the bone marrow normally is controlled by a physiological feedback mechanism analogous to the thermostatic control of temperature in a room. The mechanism is triggered by a reduction of oxygen in the tissues (hypoxia) and operates through the action of the hormone erythropoietin in the formation of which the kidney plays an important role. Erythropoietin is released and stimulates further erythropoiesis. When oxygen needs are satisfied, erythropoietin production is reduced and red cell production diminishes.

In disease, as well as in certain situations in which physiological adjustments take place, the quantity of hemoglobin may be reduced below normal levels, a condition known as anemia. It may also be increased above normal, leading to polycythemia (also called erythrocytosis).

ANEMIA

Anemia is a condition in which the red blood cells are reduced in number or volume or are deficient in hemoglobin, their oxygen-carrying pigment. Thus, in anemia the blood is capable of carrying only a reduced amount of oxygen to tissues, a condition that stimulates the lungs to increase the respiratory rate to pick up more oxygen and the heart to increase its rate to increase the volume of blood delivered to the tissues. The bone marrow normally is capable of increasing production of red cells as much as sixfold to eightfold through an increased rate of development from their primitive precursors. Anemia ensues when the normal fine balance between production, destruction, and physiological loss is upset and erythropoiesis has not been accelerated to a degree sufficient to reestablish normal blood values. The bone marrow responds to increased destruction of red cells by increasing the rate of their production.

Anemia varies in severity, as does the tolerance of different persons for anemia, depending in part on the rate at which it has developed. When anemia has developed gradually, affected persons may endure severe grades of anemia with few or no symptoms, whereas rapidly developing anemia causes severe symptoms. If sufficiently severe and rapid in development, anemia can be fatal. The most noticeable symptom of anemia is usually pallor of the skin, mucous membranes, and nail beds. Persons with anemia caused by increased destruction of red cells appear to be slightly jaundiced. Symptoms of tissue oxygen deficiency include pulsating noises in the ear, dizziness, fainting, and shortness of breath. Compensatory action of the heart may lead to its enlargement and a rapid pulse rate. There are close to 100 different varieties of anemia, distinguished by the cause and the size and hemoglobin content of the abnormal cells.

Increased destruction of red blood cells (hemolysis) may be caused by hereditary cell defects, as in sickle cell anemia, hereditary spherocytosis, or glucose-6-phosphate dehydrogenase deficiency. Destruction also may be caused by exposure to hemolytic chemicals (substances causing the release of hemoglobin from the red cells) such as the antibiotic drug sulfanilamide, the antimalarial drug primaquine, or naphthalene (mothballs), or it may be caused by development of antibodies against the red blood cells, as in erythroblastosis fetalis. Reduced production of red cells may be caused by disorders of the bone marrow, as in leukemia and aplastic anemia, or by deficiency of one or more of the nutrients—notably vitamin B_{12}, folic acid (folate), and iron—that are necessary for the synthesis of red cells. Lower production may also be caused by deficiency of certain hormones or inhibition of the red cell–forming processes by certain drugs or by toxins produced by disease, particularly chronic infection, cancer, and kidney failure. In addition, reduced red blood cell numbers may occur as a result of blood loss caused by trauma or certain conditions such as peptic ulcer.

Structurally, the anemias generally fall into the following four types: (1) macrocytic anemia, characterized by larger-than-normal red cells and caused by impaired production of red cells, such as when vitamin B_{12} or folic acid is lacking (e.g., pernicious anemia); (2) normocytic anemia, characterized by a decrease in the number of red cells, which are otherwise relatively normal, typically with no significant alteration in the size, shape, or coloration of the red cells (e.g., anemia caused by sudden blood loss, as in a bleeding peptic ulcer, most cases of hemophilia, and purpura); (3) simple microcytic anemia, characterized by smaller-than-normal red cells (encountered in cases of chronic inflammatory conditions and in renal disease); and (4) microcytic hypochromic anemia, characterized by a reduction in red-cell size and hemoglobin concentration (frequently associated with iron deficiency anemia but also seen in thalassemia).

Diagnosis of the type of anemia is based on patient history and physical examination, which may reveal an underlying cause, and on examination of the blood. The latter includes measurement of the degree of anemia and microscopic study of the red cells. If the number of red cells, the hemoglobin concentration of the blood, and the volume of packed red cells are known, the mean volume and hemoglobin content can be calculated. The mean corpuscular volume (MCV) normally is 82 to 92 cubic micrometres, and about one-third of this is hemoglobin (mean corpuscular hemoglobin concentration, or MCHC, normally is 32 to 36 percent). If determined accurately, the MCV and the MCHC are useful indexes of the nature of an anemia. Accurate diagnosis is essential before treatment is attempted because, just as the causes differ widely, the treatment of anemia differs from one patient to another. Indiscriminate treatment by the use of hematinics (drugs that stimulate production of red cells or hemoglobin) can be dangerous.

The treatment of anemia varies depending on the diagnosis. It includes supplying the missing nutrients in the deficiency anemias, detecting and removing toxic factors, improving the underlying disorder with drugs and other forms of therapy, decreasing the extent of blood destruction by methods that include surgery (e.g., splenectomy), or restoring blood volume with transfusion.

MEGALOBLASTIC ANEMIAS

Megaloblastic anemia, the production in the bone marrow of abnormal nucleated red cells known as megaloblasts, develops as the result of dietary deficiency of, faulty absorption of, or increased demands for vitamin B$_{12}$ or folic acid. When such a vitamin deficiency occurs, bone marrow activity is seriously impaired. Marrow cells proliferate but do not mature properly, and erythropoiesis becomes largely ineffective. Anemia develops, the number of young red cells (reticulocytes) is reduced, and even the numbers of granulocytes (white cells that contain granules in the cellular substance outside the nucleus) and platelets are decreased. The mature red cells that are formed from megaloblasts are larger than normal, resulting in a macrocytic anemia. The impaired and ineffective erythropoiesis is associated with accelerated destruction of the red cells, thereby providing the features of a hemolytic anemia (caused by the destruction of red cells at a rate substantially greater than normal).

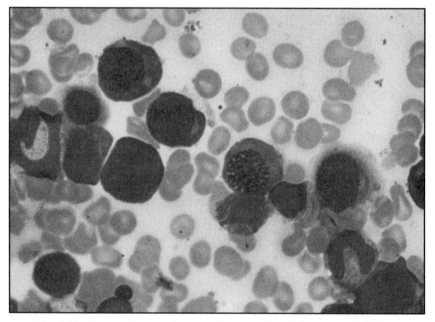

Megaloblastic anemia occurs because of vitamin B$_{12}$ deficiency or malabsorption. The condition is named for the abnormally large red blood cells it produces known as megaloblasts. © OJ Staats/Custom Medical Stock Photo

Vitamin B_{12} is a red, cobalt-containing vitamin that is found in animal foods and is important in the synthesis of DNA. A deficiency of vitamin B_{12} leads to disordered production of DNA and hence to the impaired production of red cells. Unlike other vitamins, it is formed not by higher plants but only by certain bacteria and molds and in the rumen (first stomach chamber) of sheep and cattle, provided that traces of cobalt are present in their fodder. In humans, vitamin B_{12} must be obtained passively, by eating food of an animal source. Furthermore, this vitamin is not absorbed efficiently from the human intestinal tract unless a certain secretion of the stomach, intrinsic factor, is available to bind with vitamin B_{12}.

The most common cause of vitamin B_{12} deficiency is pernicious anemia, a condition mostly affecting elderly persons. In this disorder the stomach does not secrete intrinsic factor, perhaps as the result of an immune process consisting of the production of antibodies directed against the stomach lining. The tendency to form such antibodies may be hereditary. Patients with pernicious anemia are given monthly injections of vitamin B_{12}. Oral treatment with the vitamin is possible but inefficient because absorption is poor.

Other forms of vitamin B_{12} deficiency are rare. They are seen in complete vegetarians (vegans) whose diets lack vitamin B_{12}, in persons whose stomachs have been completely removed and so lack a source of intrinsic factor, in those who are infected with the fish tapeworm *Diphyllobothrium latum* or have intestinal cul-de-sacs or partial obstructions where competition by the tapeworms or by bacteria for vitamin B_{12} deprives the host, and in persons with primary intestinal diseases that affect the absorptive capacity of the small intestine (ileum). In these conditions, additional nutritional deficiencies, such as of folic acid and iron, are also likely to develop.

Blood changes similar to those occurring in vitamin B_{12} deficiency result from deficiency of folic acid. Folic acid (folate) is a vitamin found in leafy vegetables, but it is also synthesized by certain intestinal bacteria. Deficiency usually is the result of a highly defective diet or of chronic intestinal malabsorption. Pregnancy greatly increases the need for this vitamin. There is also an increased demand in cases of chronic accelerated production of red cells. This type of deficiency also has been observed in some patients receiving anticonvulsant drugs, and there is some evidence that absorption of the vitamin may be impaired in these cases. Often several factors affecting supply and demand of the vitamin play a role in producing folic acid deficiency. Unless folic acid deficiency is complicated by the presence of intestinal or liver disease, its treatment rarely requires more than the institution of a normal diet. In any event, the oral administration of folic acid relieves the megaloblastic anemia. Some effect can be demonstrated even in pernicious anemia, but this treatment is unsafe because the nervous system is not protected against the effects of vitamin B_{12} deficiency, and serious damage to the nervous system may occur unless vitamin B_{12} is given.

In addition to the aforementioned conditions, megaloblastic anemia may arise in still other situations. Selective vitamin B_{12} malabsorption may be the consequence of a hereditary defect. Deranged metabolism may play a role in some instances of megaloblastic anemia that accompany pregnancy. Metabolic antagonism is thought to be the mechanism underlying the megaloblastic anemia associated with the use of certain anticonvulsant drugs and some drugs employed in the treatment of leukemia and other forms of cancer. In fact, one of the earliest drugs used to treat leukemia was a folic acid antagonist.

PERNICIOUS ANEMIA

Pernicious anemia is a disease in which the production of red blood cells is impaired because the body cannot absorb vitamin B_{12}, which is necessary for red blood cells to mature properly in the bone marrow. Pernicious anemia is one of many types of anemia, a disease marked by a reduction in red blood cells or in the oxygen-carrying substance hemoglobin found in those cells. Symptoms of pernicious anemia include weakness, waxy pallor, shortness of breath, rapid heartbeat, unsteady gait, smooth tongue, gastrointestinal disturbances, and neurological problems. Pernicious anemia is in most cases associated with an inflammation of the stomach called autoimmune gastritis. An absence of hydrochloric acid in gastric secretions (achlorhydria) is also characteristic of pernicious anemia. The anemia may become severe before the disorder is diagnosed, because the vitamin deficiency develops very gradually.

In pernicious anemia vitamin B_{12} is unavailable because of the lack of intrinsic factor. In a healthy person intrinsic factor is produced by the parietal cells of the stomach, the cells that also secrete hydrochloric acid. Intrinsic factor forms a complex with dietary vitamin B_{12} in the stomach. This complex remains intact, preventing degradation of the vitamin by intestinal juices, until it reaches the ileum of the small intestine, where the vitamin is released and absorbed into the body. When intrinsic factor is prevented from binding with vitamin B_{12} or when the parietal cells are unable to produce intrinsic factor, the vitamin is not absorbed and pernicious anemia results. This is believed to stem from an autoimmune reaction in which the malfunctioning immune system produces antibodies against intrinsic factor and against the parietal cells.

With an inadequate amount of vitamin B_{12}, the body is unable to synthesize DNA properly. This in turn affects red blood cell production: the cells divide, but their nuclei remain immature. These cells, called megaloblasts, are for the most part destroyed in the bone marrow and not released to the circulation. Some megaloblasts mature to become large red blood cells called macrocytes, which reach the circulation but function abnormally. A deficiency of white blood cells (leukopenia) and of platelets (thrombocytopenia) is also seen in the blood.

Pernicious anemia occurs most often in persons older than age 30 years, but a juvenile form of the disease does occur, usually in children younger than age 3. The disease shows a familial tendency and is more common in individuals of northern European descent.

Treatment involves a monthly intramuscular injection of vitamin B_{12} that must be continued for life. Most patients improve quickly, but neurological damage is seldom fully reversible and atrophy of the parietal cells and achlorhydria persist. Before the discovery of treatment in the 1920s, the modifier *pernicious*, although something of a misnomer today, was appropriate, because the disease was usually fatal.

NORMOCYTIC NORMOCHROMIC ANEMIAS

Forms of anemia in which the average size and hemoglobin content of the red blood cells are within normal limits are called normocytic normochromic anemias. Usually microscopic examination of the red cells shows them to be much like normal cells. In other cases there may be marked variations in size and shape, but these are such as to equalize one another, thus resulting in normal average values. The normocytic anemias are a miscellaneous group, by no means as homogeneous as the megaloblastic anemias.

Anemia caused by the sudden loss of blood is necessarily normocytic at first, because the cells that remain in the circulation are normal. The blood loss stimulates increased production, and the young cells that enter the blood in response are larger than those already present in the blood. If the young cells are present in sufficient number, the anemia temporarily becomes macrocytic (but not megaloblastic). Treatment of anemia caused by sudden blood loss includes transfusion.

A common form of anemia is that occurring in association with various chronic infections and in a variety of chronic systemic diseases. As a rule the anemia is not severe, but the anemia associated with chronic renal insufficiency (defective functioning of the kidneys) may be extremely so. Most normocytic anemias appear to be the result of impaired production of red cells, and in renal failure there is a deficiency of erythropoietin, the factor in the body that normally stimulates red cell production. In these states, the life span of the red cell in the circulation may be slightly shortened, but the cause of the anemia is failure of red cell production. The anemia associated with chronic disorders is characterized by abnormally low levels of iron in the plasma and excessive quantities in the reticuloendothelial cells (cells whose function is ingestion and destruction of other cells and of foreign particles) of the bone marrow. Successful treatment depends on eliminating or relieving the underlying disorder.

The mild anemias associated with deficiencies of anterior pituitary, thyroid, adrenocortical, or testicular hormones usually are normocytic. As in the case of anemia associated with chronic infections or various systemic diseases, the symptoms usually are those of the underlying condition, but sometimes anemia may be the most prominent sign. Unless complicated by deficiencies of vitamin

B$_{12}$ or iron, these anemias are cured by appropriate treatment with the deficient hormone.

Invasion of bone marrow by cancer cells carried by the bloodstream, if sufficiently great, is accompanied by anemia, usually normocytic in type but associated with abnormalities of both red and white cells. It is thought that such anemia is caused by impaired production of red cells through mechanical interference. Whether this is true or not, a characteristic sign in the peripheral blood is the appearance of many irregularities in the size and shape of the red cells and of nucleated red cells. These young cells normally never leave the bone marrow but appear when the structure of the marrow is distorted by invading cells.

APLASTIC ANEMIA

Aplastic anemia is a disease in which the bone marrow fails to produce an adequate number of blood cells. There may be a lack of all cell types—white blood cells, red blood cells, and platelets—resulting in a form of the disease called pancytopenia, or there may be a lack of one or more cell types. Rarely, the disease may be congenital (Fanconi anemia). More commonly, it is acquired by exposure to certain drugs (e.g., the antibiotic chloramphenicol) or chemicals (e.g., benzene) or to ionizing radiation. About half of all cases are idiopathic (cause unknown). Aplastic anemia is most common in persons 15 to 30 years of age.

In aplastic anemia the normally red marrow becomes fatty and yellow and fails to form enough red cells, white cells, and platelets. Anemia with few or no reticulocytes, reduced levels of the types of white cells formed in the bone marrow (granulocytes), and reduced platelets in the blood are characteristic of this condition.

Manifestations of aplastic anemia are related to the various resulting blood cell deficiencies and include weakness, increased susceptibility to infections, and bleeding. Onset of the disease may be abrupt, quickly becoming severe and possibly fatal. More commonly, it is insidious, running a chronic course of several years. Symptoms of chronic aplastic anemia include weakness and fatigue in the early stages, followed by shortness of breath, headache, fever, and pounding heart. There is usually a waxy pallor, and hemorrhages occur in the mucous membranes, skin, and other organs. If white blood cells (specifically, neutrophils) are lacking, resistance to infection is much lowered and infection becomes the major cause of death. When platelets are very low, bleeding may be severe.

In some cases the onset of aplastic anemia has been found to have been preceded by exposure to such organic chemicals as benzol, insecticides, or a variety of drugs, especially the antibiotic chloramphenicol. Although it is well established that certain agents may produce aplastic anemia, most persons exposed to these agents do not develop the disease, and most persons with aplastic anemia have no clear history of exposure to such agents.

There are other agents that produce aplastic anemia in a predictable way. These include some of the chemotherapeutic agents used in the treatment of cancer, lymphoma, and leukemia, as well as radiation treatment for these diseases. Because of this fact, blood counts are frequently checked and doses of drugs or radiation are modified in patients being treated. Withdrawal of medication is followed by recovery of the bone marrow in such cases. Converely, in those patients who develop aplastic anemia as a result of exposure to other toxic agents, cessation of exposure may not result in recovery of the marrow, or at best the marrow may be indolent and incomplete.

Treatment of aplastic anemia is a twofold process. First, complications of the disease must be treated: infection calls for vigorous treatment with antibiotics; symptoms caused by anemia call for red cell transfusions; and bleeding calls for platelet transfusions. Second, efforts should be directed toward inducing bone marrow recovery. Based on the hypothesis that one of the mechanisms of production of the aplastic anemia is autoimmunity, medication to suppress the immune response, such as the administration of antithymocyte globulin, is occasionally successful. An important and effective treatment is transplantation of bone marrow from a normal, compatible donor, usually a sibling. This treatment is limited by the availability of compatible donors and also by the fact that the recipient is increasingly prone to serious complications with advancing age. If transplantation is not practical, treatment involves avoidance of the toxic agent if known, supportive care (administration of fluids, glucose, and proteins, often intravenously), transfusions of blood components, and administration of antibiotics. Spontaneous recovery occurs occasionally.

HYPOCHROMIC MICROCYTIC ANEMIAS

Hypochromic microcytic anemias, characterized by the presence in the circulating blood of red cells that are smaller than normal and poorly filled with hemoglobin, fall into two main categories. The first is a result of a deficiency of iron, and the second is a result of impaired production of hemoglobin. In either case, there is an inadequate amount of the final product in the red cell.

Small red blood cells poorly filled with hemoglobin are characteristic of a hereditary disorder of hemoglobin formation, thalassemia, that is common among Mediterranean peoples. With the exception of iron deficiency and thalassemia, hypochromic microcytic anemia is rare. It is seen in anemia responsive to vitamin B_6 (pyridoxine), where the anemia probably results from a metabolic fault in the synthesis of the heme portion of hemoglobin. Sideroblastic anemia, characterized by the presence in the bone marrow of nucleated red blood cells, the nucleus of which is surrounded by a ring of iron granules (ringed sideroblasts) and by a proportion of small, pale red cells in the blood, is of unknown cause and difficult to treat.

Iron Deficiency Anemia

Iron deficiency anemia develops because of a lack of the mineral iron, the main function of which is in the formation of hemoglobin, the blood pigment that carries oxygen from the blood to the tissues. Iron deficiency is the most common cause of anemia throughout the world. It is estimated that iron deficiency anemia affects approximately 15 percent of the population worldwide.

Iron is required for hemoglobin formation. If the supply is insufficient to produce normal quantities of hemoglobin, the bone marrow ultimately is forced to produce cells that are smaller than normal and poorly filled with hemoglobin. Iron is derived from the diet and absorbed in the intestinal tract. Once in the body, it is retained and used over and over again, only minimal amounts being lost through shedding of cells from the skin and the exposed membranes and, in the female, through normal menstruation.

In the adult the body iron content is approximately 3.7 grams, of which more than half is hemoglobin. In the male there is virtually no further need for iron. Deficiency results if the dietary supplies of iron are insufficient to meet the needs; if absorption is faulty, as in malabsorption disorders; or if blood loss is occurring. Common causes of iron deficiency are excessive menstrual loss in women and bleeding peptic ulcer in men. Iron deficiency is common in infancy and childhood because demands are great for the ever-expanding pool of circulating hemoglobin in the growing body, and in pregnancy when the fetus must be

"The anemic lady," painted by Dutch artist Samuel van Hoogstraten circa 1667. Iron deficiency was once so common a malady that it was frequently depicted in literature and art. © Christie's Images Ltd./SuperStock

supplied with iron. Hookworm infestation is a common cause of iron deficiency where conditions for the worm are favourable, because the intestinal blood loss caused by the myriad worms attached to the wall is great.

People with iron deficiency anemia are pale but not jaundiced. Other symptoms include weakness, fatigue, shortness of breath, coldness of extremities, changeable appetite, sore tongue, loss of hair, brittle fingernails, or dry skin. Under the name of chlorosis, this type of anemia was mentioned in popular literature and depicted in paintings, especially those of the Dutch masters, until the 20th century. Although it is not necessarily less common now, there is no doubt that it is less severe in Europe and North America than it once was. The only treatment required is oral administration of iron salts in some palatable form, such as ferrous sulfate. Quick improvement is common.

HEMOLYTIC ANEMIAS

Destruction of red cells at a rate substantially greater than normal, if not compensated for by accelerated red cell production, causes hemolytic anemia. Increased red cell destruction is recognized by demonstrating increased quantities of the pigmentary products of their destruction, such as bilirubin and urobilinogen, in the blood plasma, urine, and feces and by evidence of accelerated erythropoiesis, such as an increase in the number of young cells (reticulocytes) in the blood. When blood cell destruction is extremely rapid or occurs in the blood vessels, free hemoglobin is found in the urine (hemoglobinuria). Treatment varies with the cause of the hemolytic anemia.

There are two principal causes of hemolytic anemia: (1) inherently defective red cells and (2) an environment hostile to red cells. Abnormalities within the red cell are usually congenital and hereditary. They are exemplified by diseases in which the cell membrane is weakened, cell metabolism is defective, or hemoglobin is abnormal.

Hereditary spherocytosis is the most common disease involving the red cell membrane. It is characterized by the presence of red cells that appear small, stain densely for hemoglobin, and look nearly spherical. Such cells are mechanically fragile and readily swell up and burst in dilute salt solution. In the body they break up when deprived of free access to plasma glucose. The abnormality is aggravated by a tendency for the cells to remain longer than usual in the spleen because of their spheroidal shape. The corpuscular defect may appear if it is inherited from either parent (it is caused by a dominant gene). The anemia varies in severity. It may be so mild as to pass unnoticed for years, but it may suddenly become severe—e.g., when an incidental respiratory infection briefly suppresses the accelerated production of red cells necessary to meet the constantly increased rate of their destruction. Parvovirus is known to cause this transient cessation of erythropoiesis, and the development of severe anemia under these circumstances is termed aplastic crisis. Removal of the spleen, which always is enlarged, cures the anemia by eliminating the site of sequestration and destruction of the red blood cells but does not prevent hereditary transmission of the disease.

Red cells metabolize glucose by breaking it down to lactic acid either via an anaerobic (oxygenless) pathway or by oxidation through a pathway called the pentose phosphate pathway. The anaerobic pathway, the main route of metabolism, provides energy in the form of adenosine triphosphate (ATP). Deficiencies of enzymes such as pyruvate kinase in this pathway shorten red cell survival times because energy-requiring activities within the red cell are curtailed. Deficiencies of enzymes in the anaerobic pathway are generally relevant only when they are homozygous (i.e., when the deficiency is inherited from each parent on an autosomal chromosome and is therefore expressed). Abnormalities also have been discovered in the alternative process of glucose metabolism, the pentose phosphate pathway. Deficiency of the first enzyme in the pathway, glucose-6-phosphate dehydrogenase (G-6-PD), is rather common. This deficiency results in destruction of red cells (hemolysis). G-6-PD deficiency occurs in 10 to 14 percent of African Americans; the defect is harmless unless the person is exposed to certain drugs, such as certain antimalarial compounds (e.g., primaquine) and sulfonamides. The full effect of the deficiency is rarely observed in females because the gene is sex-linked (i.e., carried on the X chromosome), and only rarely do both X chromosomes carry the abnormal gene. Males, on the other hand, have only one X chromosome and thus only one gene available, and therefore the deficiency is fully expressed if it is inherited on the X chromosome from the mother. Another variety of G-6-PD deficiency is especially frequent in persons of Mediterranean descent.

Hemolytic anemia can also result as the consequence of an environment hostile to the red cell. Certain chemical agents destroy red cells whenever sufficient amounts are given (e.g., phenylhydrazine); others are harmful only to persons whose red cells are sensitive to the action of the agent. A number of toxic drugs are oxidants or are transformed into oxidizing substances in the body. Injury may be accidental, as with moth ball (naphthalene) ingestion in children, or it may be the undesirable effect of a drug used therapeutically. Individual sensitivity is of several kinds. Certain patients are susceptible to oxidant drugs such as antimalarial compounds. This is attributable to a sex-linked, inherited deficiency of the enzyme G-6-PD. In other instances, sensitivity is on an immunologic basis (e.g., hemolytic anemia caused by administration of penicillin or quinidine). The anemia develops rapidly over a few days and may be fatal without transfusions.

A long-recognized type of hemolytic anemia is that associated with the transfusion of incompatible red cells. Antibodies to the substances alpha- and beta-isoagglutinin, which occur naturally in the blood, destroy the donor red cells when incompatible blood is given by transfusion. Besides the best-known blood groups — A, B, and O — there are other groups to which a person may develop antibodies that will cause transfusion reactions. The rhesus (Rh) and Kell groups are examples. In erythroblastosis fetalis (hemolytic disease of the newborn), the destruction of fetal blood by that of the mother may be due to Rh or ABO incompatibility. The events that take place are, first, the passage of incompatible red cells from the fetus into the circulation of the mother through a break in the placental blood vessels, then development of antibodies in the mother, and, finally, passage of these antibodies into the fetus, with consequent hemolysis, anemia, and jaundice.

A form of hemolytic anemia that is relatively common depends on the formation of antibodies within the patient's body against his own red cells (autoimmune hemolytic anemia). This may occur in association with the presence of certain diseases, but it is often seen without other illness. Trapping of the red cells by the spleen is thought to depend on the fact that, when brought into contact with reticuloendothelial cells, red cells coated with incomplete (nonhemolytic) antibody adhere, become spherical, are ingested (phagocytosed), and break down.

Such anemias may be severe but often can be controlled by the administration of adrenocorticosteroids (which interfere with the destructive process) and treatment of the underlying disease, if one is present. In a number of instances, splenectomy—removal of the spleen—is necessary and is usually partially or wholly effective in relieving the anemia. The effectiveness of splenectomy is attributed to the removal of the organ in which red cells, coated with antibody, are selectively trapped and destroyed.

Other varieties of hemolytic anemia include that associated with mechanical trauma, such as that produced by the impact of red cells on artificial heart valves, excessive heat, and infectious agents (e.g., the organism causing malaria).

HEMOGLOBINOPATHY

Hemoglobinopathy is any of a group of disorders caused by the presence of variant hemoglobin in the red blood cells. Hemoglobin is composed of a porphyrin compound (heme) and globin. Normal adult hemoglobin (Hb A) consists of globin containing two pairs of polypeptide chains, alpha (α) and beta (β). A minor fraction of normal adult hemoglobin consists of Hb A$_2$, which contains α- and delta- (δ-) chains. A different hemoglobin (Hb F) is present in fetal life and possesses a pair of the same α-chains as does Hb A, but the second set contains gamma- (γ-) chains. In normal hemoglobin, the order in which the amino acids follow one another in the polypeptide chain is always exactly the same.

A malfunction of the abnormal hemoglobin may result in erythrocythemia, or overproduction of red cells. In these cases there is increased oxygen affinity, limiting proper delivery of oxygen to tissues and thereby stimulating the bone marrow to increase red cell production. In other cases the iron in heme may exist in the oxidized, or ferric (Fe^{3+}), state and thus cannot combine with oxygen to carry it to tissues. This results in a bluish colour of the skin and mucous membranes (cyanosis). The abnormality in the globin molecule that accounts for this is usually in an area of the molecule called the heme pocket, which normally protects the iron against oxidation, despite the fact that oxygen is being carried at this site.

Variant-hemoglobin disorders occur geographically throughout the Old World in a beltlike area roughly the same as that of malaria. The presence of variant hemoglobin in moderate amounts may constitute a selective advantage in that it provides some protection from the lethal effects of malaria, thereby allowing more persons to reach reproductive age. The most important of the hemoglobinopathies are sickle cell anemia and thalassemia. Hemoglobin C (Hb C) is relatively common among African blacks living north of the Niger River and is found in 2–3 percent of blacks in the United States. Hemoglobin C disease (occurring when the variant Hb C gene is inherited from both parents) produces such symptoms and signs as vague pain, jaundice, enlarged spleen, mild to moderate anemia, and some hemorrhaging. The life span of the individual, however, is normal, and the disease is much milder than the sickle cell anemia found in the same geographic range. It is possible that Hb C is gradually replacing Hb S (variant hemoglobin of sickle cell anemia) by a process of selection in Africa. Although Hb C does not produce early mortality in homozygotes (persons with two genes for Hb C), as does sickle cell anemia, it may afford some protection from malaria.

Hemoglobin D is found mainly in people of Afghan, Pakistani, and northwestern Indian descent, but it also occurs in those of European ancestry. Hemoglobin D disease (two genes for Hb D) may produce mild hemolytic anemia. Hemoglobin E is widespread in Southeast Asia, being found especially among Thai, Cambodian, Laotian, Malaysian, Indonesian, Vietnamese, and Burmese peoples. Hemoglobin E disease (two genes for Hb E) may result in a mild microcytic (small red blood cell) anemia. Hemoglobin E–thalassemia disease (one gene for Hb E, one gene for thalassemia) is severe and clinically closely resembles thalassemia major. Hemoglobin H, found in many groups in the Old World (e.g., Chinese, Thai, Malayans, Greeks, Italians), has almost always been identified in combination with thalassemia, and symptoms resemble those of thalassemia. Many other variant hemoglobins—such as types G, J, K, L, N, O, P, Q, and variants of Hb A ("normal" hemoglobin) and Hb F (fetal hemoglobin)—are known but typically do not produce clinical manifestations.

In sickle cell anemia and other abnormalities of hemoglobin (hemoglobinopathy), the substitution of one amino acid for another at a particular site in the chain is the underlying cause. The substitution of valyl for glutamyl in the sixth position of the β-chain, for example, results in the formation of Hb S (the hemoglobin of sickle cell disease) instead of Hb A. This variant hemoglobin is inherited as a Mendelian recessive trait. Thus, if only one parent transmits the gene for Hb S, the offspring inherits the trait but is harmed relatively little. The red cells contain more Hb A than Hb S. If the trait is inherited from both parents, the predominant hemoglobin in the red cell is Hb S, resulting in the serious and sometimes fatal disease sickle cell anemia. There also may occur combinations of hemoglobin abnormalities, or different hemoglobin abnormalities may be inherited from each parent. For example, sickle-thalassemia and Hb E-thalassemia are relatively common.

Since the first characterization of the nature of Hb S by American chemist Linus Pauling and his associates in 1949, more than 100 variant hemoglobins have been identified. Fortunately, most variant hemoglobins are insufficiently affected to alter their function, and therefore no observable illness occurs.

Thalassemia

Thalassemia is a group of blood disorders characterized by a deficiency of hemoglobin. Hemoglobin is composed of a porphyrin compound (heme) and globin. Thalassemia is caused by genetically determined abnormalities in the synthesis of one or more of the polypeptide chains of globin. The various forms of the disorder are distinguished by different combinations of three variables: the particular polypeptide chain or chains that are affected; whether the affected chains are synthesized in sharply reduced quantities or not synthesized at all; and whether the disorder is inherited from one parent (heterozygous) or from both parents (homozygous).

The five different polypeptide chains are alpha, α; beta, β; gamma, γ; delta, δ; and epsilon, ε. No thalassemic disorder is known to involve the ε-chain. Involvement of the γ-chain or δ-chain is rare. Of the 19 variations of thalassemic inheritance, a few (such as the two heterozygous α-thalassemias) are benign and generally exhibit no clinical symptoms. Other forms exhibit mild anemia, whereas the most severe form (homozygous α-thalassemia) usually causes premature birth, either stillborn or with death following within a few hours. It is thought that a primary thalassemia genetic mutation results in reduction in the rate at which α-, β-, or δ-chains are manufactured, the chains being otherwise normal. The relative deficiency of one pair of chains and the resultant imbalance of chain pairs result in ineffective production of red blood cells, deficient hemoglobin production, microcytosis (small cells), and destruction of red cells (hemolysis).

When defects occur in both δ- and β-chain synthesis, causing δ-β-thalassemia, Hb F concentrations usually are considerably elevated because the number of β-chains available to combine with α-chains is limited and γ-chain synthesis is not impaired. Beta-thalassemia comprises most thalassemias. A number of genetic mechanisms account for impaired production of β-chains, all of which result in inadequate supplies of messenger RNA (mRNA) available for proper synthesis of the β-chain at the ribosome. In some cases no mRNA is produced. Most defects have to do with production and processing of the RNA from the β-gene. In α-thalassemia, by contrast, the gene is deleted. There are normally two pairs of α-genes, and the severity of the anemia is determined by the number deleted. Because all normal hemoglobins contain α-chains, there is no increase in Hb F or Hb A_1. The extra non–α-chains may combine into tetramers to form $β_4$ (hemoglobin H) or $γ_4$ (hemoglobin Bart). These tetramers are unstable and ineffective in delivering oxygen. Inheritance of deficiency of a pair of genes from both parents results in intrauterine fetal death or severe disease of the newborn.

Thalassemia (Greek for "sea blood") is so called because it was first discovered among peoples around the Mediterranean Sea, among whom its incidence is high. Thalassemia now is also common in Thailand and elsewhere in the Far East. The potentially lethal thalassemia gene likely is retained in the population because it provides some protection from malaria in the heterozygous state. Thalassemia genes are widely distributed in the world but are found most often among people with ancestors from the Mediterranean, the Middle East, and southern Asia. Thalassemia has also been found in some northern Europeans and Native Americans. Among persons of African descent, the disease is unusually mild.

The red cells in this condition are unusually flat with central staining areas and thus have been called target cells. In the mild form of the disease, thalassemia minor (heterozygous β-thalassemia), there is usually only slight or no anemia, and life expectancy is normal. Occasionally, complications occur involving slight enlargement of the spleen. Thalassemia major (homozygous β-thalassemia, or Cooley anemia) is characterized by severe anemia, enlargement of the spleen, and body deformities associated with expansion of the bone marrow. The latter presumably represents a response to the need for greatly accelerated red cell production by genetically defective red cell precursors, which are relatively ineffective in producing mature red cells. Clinical characteristics of thalassemia major, including anemia, enlarged spleen, and often enlarged liver, appear a few months following birth. Infections commonly develop. At about the age of four years, stunted physical growth becomes apparent. Many patients develop abnormally protruding upper jaws, prominent cheekbones, and marrow expansion in the long bones, ribs, or vertebrae, which fracture easily. Treatment of thalassemia major involves blood transfusions, but they are of only temporary value and lead to excessive iron in the tissues once the transfused red cells break down. The enlarged spleen may further aggravate the anemia by pooling and trapping the circulating red cells. Splenectomy may partially relieve the anemia but does not cure the disease.

Sickle Cell Anemia

Sickle cell anemia is a hereditary disease that destroys red blood cells by causing them to take on a rigid "sickle" shape. The disease is characterized by many of the symptoms of chronic anemia (fatigue, pale skin, and shortness of breath) as well as susceptibility to infection; jaundice and other eye problems; delayed growth; and episodic crises of severe pain in the abdomen, bones, or muscles. Sickle cell anemia occurs mainly in persons of African descent but also occurs in persons of the Middle East, the Mediterranean, and India.

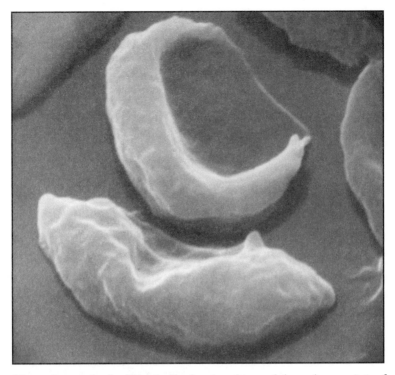

Photomicrograph of red blood cells, showing abnormal shape characteristic of sickle cell anemia. NASA

Sickle cell anemia is caused by a variant type of hemoglobin, the protein in red blood cells that carries oxygen to the tissues of the body, called hemoglobin S (Hb S). Hb S is sensitive to deficiency of oxygen. When the carrier red blood cells release their oxygen to the tissues and the oxygen concentration within those cells is reduced, Hb S, unlike normal hemoglobin (Hb A), becomes stacked within the red cells in filaments that twist into helical rods. These rods then cluster into parallel bundles that distort and elongate the cells, causing them to become rigid and assume a sickle shape. This phenomenon is to some extent reversible after the cells become oxygenated once more, but repeated sickling ultimately results in irreversible distortion of the red cells. The sickle-shaped cells become clogged in small blood vessels, causing obstruction of the microcirculation, which in turn results in damage to and destruction of various tissues.

The Hb S gene is distributed geographically in a broad equatorial belt in Africa and less often in other parts of the continent and the Americas, where at least 8 percent of black Americans, or 1 in every 12, carry the sickle cell trait. The actual disease is less common (about 1 in 500 black Americans). The persistence of Hb S has been explained by the fact that heterozygous persons are resistant to malaria. When the red cells of a person with the sickle cell trait are invaded by the malarial parasite, the red cells adhere to blood vessel walls, become deoxygenated, assume the sickle shape, and then are destroyed, the parasite being destroyed with them.

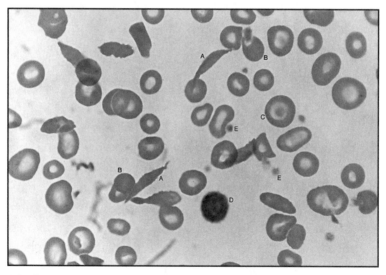

Blood smear in which the red cells show variation in size and shape typical of sickle cell anemia. (A) Long, thin, deeply stained cells with pointed ends are irreversibly sickled. (B) Small, round, dense cells are hyperchromic, because a part of the membrane is lost during sickling. (C) Target cell with a concentration of hemoglobin on its centre. (D) Lymphocyte. (E) Platelets. Encyclopædia Britannica, Inc.

If both parents have the sickle cell trait, the chances are 1 in 4 that a child born to them will develop sickle cell anemia. However, through amniocentesis (analysis of amniotic fluid surrounding a fetus), a testing procedure done in the early stages of pregnancy, it is possible to detect sickle cell anemia in the fetus. A person who inherits the sickle cell gene from one parent and a normal hemoglobin gene (Hb A) from the other parent (an inheritance known as the heterozygous state) is a carrier of the sickle cell trait. Because the red blood cells of heterozygous persons contain both Hb A and Hb S, such cells require much greater deoxygenation to produce sickling than do those of persons with sickle cell anemia. Most persons with the sickle cell trait thus have no symptoms of disease, but certain manifestations—mainly associated with vigorous exertion at high altitudes—have been seen. The overall mortality rate of persons with the sickle cell trait is no different from that of a normal comparable population.

Sickle cell anemia is characterized by severe chronic anemia punctuated by painful crises, the latter caused by blockage of the capillary beds in various organs by masses of sickled red cells. This gives rise to fever and episodic pains in the chest, abdomen, or joints that are difficult to distinguish from the effects of other diseases. Although the many complications of the disease can be treated and pain relieved, there is no treatment to reverse or prevent the actual sickling process. Most care is devoted to alleviating symptoms. Infants and young children with the disease are given regular daily doses of penicillin to prevent serious infection. In some cases blood transfusions are given regularly to prevent organ damage and stroke and to relieve the worst symptoms of red blood cell loss. In severe cases bone marrow transplantation has been of some benefit. The drug hydroxyurea reduces the principal symptoms of sickle cell anemia. Hydroxyurea apparently activates a gene that triggers the body's production of fetal hemoglobin. This type of hemoglobin, which is ordinarily produced in large amounts only by infants shortly before and after birth, does not sickle. Hydroxyurea therapy increases the proportion of fetal hemoglobin in the bloodstream of adult patients from 1 to about 20 percent, a proportion high enough to lessen markedly the circulatory problems that arise during crises.

POLYCYTHEMIA

Polycythemia is an abnormal increase in red blood cells and hemoglobin in the circulation, a situation that results in thickened blood, retarded flow, and an increased danger of clot formation within the circulatory system. The condition often results in an increased volume of packed red cells upon hematocrit analysis. Polycythemia occurs in response to some known stimulus for the production of red cells.

Polycythemia may be relative (e.g., after blood plasma loss), transient (as when a large number of red blood cells suddenly enter the circulation from storage), or absolute (i.e., reflecting an increase in actual mass of red cells in the body). Relative polycythemia may be the consequence of abnormally lowered fluid intake or of marked loss of body fluid, such as occurs in persistent vomiting, severe diarrhea, or copious sweating or when water is caused to shift from the circulation into the tissue. Relative and transient, or secondary, polycythemia disappear when the condition to which they are secondary is eliminated. Absolute polycythemia, when the cause is known, is called erythrocytosis.

Polycythemia is a response by the body to an increased demand for oxygen. It occurs when hemoglobin is unable to pick up large amounts of oxygen from the lungs (i.e., when it is not "saturated"). This may result from decreased atmospheric pressure, such as at high altitudes, or from impaired pulmonary ventilation. The sustained increase in red cells in persons who reside permanently at high altitudes is a direct result of the diminished oxygen pressure in the environment. Chronic pulmonary disease (e.g., emphysema—abnormal distension of the lungs with air) may produce chronic hypoxemia (reduced oxygen tension in the blood) and lead to absolute polycythemia. Extreme obesity also may severely impair pulmonary ventilation and thereby cause absolute polycythemia (pickwickian syndrome).

Congenital heart disorders that permit shunting of blood from its normal path through the pulmonary circuit, thereby preventing adequate aeration of the blood, can also cause polycythemia, as can a defect in the circulating hemoglobin. The latter defect may be congenital because of an enzymatic or a hemoglobin abnormality. It may be acquired as the result of the excessive use of coal tar derivatives, such as phenacetin, which convert hemoglobin to pigments incapable of carrying oxygen (methemoglobin, sulfhemoglobin). Lastly, polycythemia can develop in the presence of certain types of tumours and as the result of the action of adrenocortical secretions. Treatment of polycythemia resulting from any of these causes involves the correction or alleviation of the primary abnormality.

Polycythemia differs from a disease called polycythemia vera (erythremia, or primary polycythemia) in which an increased amount of red cells are produced without a known cause. In polycythemia vera there is usually an increase in other blood elements as well. For example, the number of red cells and often also the numbers of white cells and platelets increase, and the spleen usually enlarges. In this disease the stem cell precursor of the bone marrow cells produces excessive progeny. Persons with polycythemia vera have an exceptionally ruddy complexion, with red discoloration of the face and sometimes the extremities, and may have headaches, dizziness, a feeling of fullness, difficulty in breathing, skin changes (e.g., tendency to bruise), and an enlarged spleen. Because of the excessive quantities of red cells, the blood is usually thick, and its flow is retarded. Sometimes it clots in the blood vessels (thrombosis) of the heart, the brain, or the extremities with serious consequences. However, because certain blood-clotting factors are not produced in adequate amounts, hemorrhages may occur from ulcers or minor wounds. Duodenal ulcer and gout occur with increased frequency in persons with polycythemia vera. The disease is relatively common in Jews, affects men more often than women, and usually appears at middle age or later.

Treatment for polycythemia vera is aimed at reducing the volume of red blood cells. One of the simplest methods is to remove the blood, one pint at a time, from a vein until the cellular level approaches normal and the symptoms disappear. Occasionally it may be necessary to use drugs or radiation therapy, in the form of radioactive phosphorus, to restrain the overactivity of the marrow cells. These treatments must be avoided when possible, however, because of their potential complications.

PICKWICKIAN SYNDROME

Pickwickian syndrome, also called obesity hypoventilation syndrome, is a complex condition of respiratory and circulatory symptoms associated with extreme obesity. The name originates from the fat boy depicted in Charles Dickens's *The Pickwick Papers,* who showed some of the same traits. (By some definitions, to be obese is to exceed one's ideal weight by 20 percent or more. An extremely obese person exceeds the optimum weight by a much larger percentage.) This condition often occurs in association with sleep apnea, which is another common complication of obesity.

In pickwickian syndrome the rate of breathing is chronically decreased below the normal level. Because of inadequate removal of carbon dioxide by the lungs, levels of carbon dioxide in the blood increase, leading to respiratory acidosis. In more severe instances, oxygen in the blood is also significantly reduced.

Individuals who have pickwickian syndrome often complain of slow thinking, drowsiness, and fatigue. Low blood oxygen causes the small blood vessels entering the lungs to constrict, thus increasing pressure in the vessels that supply the lungs. The elevated pressure stresses the right ventricle of the heart, ultimately causing right heart failure. Finally, excessive fluid accumulates throughout the body (peripheral edema), especially beneath the skin of the lower legs.

PORPHYRIA

Porphyria is any of a group of diseases characterized by the marked overproduction and excretion of porphyrins or of one or another of their precursors. The porphyrins are reddish constituents of heme, the deep red iron-containing pigment of hemoglobin, the oxygen-carrying protein of the red blood cells. The deposition of porphyrin compounds in body tissues, notably the skin, gives rise to a variety of symptoms, the nature of which depends on the specific compound that is abnormally metabolized.

Two main groups of porphyria are recognized: erythropoietic and hepatic. In the first, the overproduction occurs in relation to hemoglobin synthesis by cells in the bone marrow. In the second, the disturbance is in the liver.

There are two principal types of erythropoietic porphyria. In congenital erythropoietic porphyria, or Günther disease, the excretion of pinkish urine is noted shortly after birth. Later, the skin becomes fragile, and blisters may appear in body areas exposed to light. The teeth and bones are reddish brown. Anemia and enlargement of the spleen are frequently noted. The condition is thought to be transmitted as a recessive trait. In erythropoietic protoporphyria, the skin becomes inflamed and itchy after short exposures to sunlight, but usually there are no other impairments, and this form of porphyria, which is transmitted as a dominant trait, is compatible with normal life expectancy.

There are three types of hepatic porphyria. In acute intermittent porphyria, also called porphyria hepatica, affected persons have recurrent attacks of abdominal pain and vomiting, weakness or paralysis of the limbs, and psychic changes resembling hysteria. Attacks may be precipitated by a variety of drugs, including barbiturates and contraceptives and possibly alcohol. This condition is transmitted as a dominant trait. It is possibly the most common form of porphyria, with an overall incidence of approximately one per 100,000 population. People of Scandinavian, Anglo-Saxon, and German ancestry seem more susceptible than others.

A second type is variegate porphyria, wherein affected individuals suffer from chronic skin lesions that tend to heal slowly. Acute transient attacks of abdominal pain and nervous system symptoms may also be present. The condition is inherited as a dominant trait, especially common in the white population of South Africa.

Porphyria cutanea tarda symptomatica, or cutaneous porphyria, is the third type. It is more common in males and usually begins insidiously later in life, in the fourth to eighth decade. The exposed skin is fragile and sensitive to light and other factors. Liver function impairment, if the patient also suffers from chronic alcoholism, is present in most affected individuals. Abstinence, in alcoholic patients, results in marked improvement or disappearance of the porphyria. The tendency to develop this form of porphyria also appears to be inherited.

In addition to hereditary porphyria, there have also been rare instances of acquired hepatic porphyria, caused by intoxications. There is generally no specific treatment for porphyria. Therapy is aimed at alleviating the symptoms and preventing skin injury and attacks.

SULFHEMOGLOBINEMIA

The presence in the blood of sulfhemoglobin, the product of abnormal, irreversible binding of sulfur by the hemoglobin in the red blood cells, rendering them incapable of transporting oxygen, is known as sulfhemoglobinemia. The condition may result from the chronic use of such drugs as acetanilide and phenacetin. Symptoms include cyanosis (bluish discoloration of the skin and mucous membranes) and constipation. Concentrations of sulfhemoglobin sufficient to endanger life do not seem to occur clinically. The abnormal hemoglobin is removed from circulation only when the red cells are destroyed at the end of their life-span, and treatment involves detecting the causative drug and avoiding it.

METHEMOGLOBINEMIA

A decrease in the oxygen-carrying capacity of the red blood cells caused by the presence of methemoglobin in the blood is known as methemoglobinemia. The severity of the symptoms of methemoglobinemia is related to the quantity of methemoglobin present in the circulation and range from a bluish discoloration of the skin and mucous membrane to weakness, difficulty in breathing, and dizziness in the more severe cases.

The iron component of the hemoglobin of the red blood cells must be in the reduced (deoxidized) state to bind with oxygen. Methemoglobin contains the oxidized form of iron and is useless for oxygen transport. Normally, various organic catalysts or enzymes are active in keeping the iron in the reduced form. Hereditary methemoglobinemia occurs when there is an inborn defect in this enzyme system or when the hemoglobin molecule is abnormally structured (hemoglobin M) and is thereby more susceptible to oxidation of the iron component. Acquired methemoglobinemia may arise as a result of contact with certain drugs and chemicals that produce oxidant compounds in the circulation, causing the oxidation of iron to occur faster than the enzyme system can keep it in the reduced state.

Treatment of hereditary methemoglobinemia usually includes the administration of reduction compounds such as methylene blue. Acquired methemoglobinemia usually disappears spontaneously when the cause is removed.

CHAPTER 6

DISEASES OF WHITE BLOOD CELLS AND PLATELETS AND DISORDERS OF COAGULATION

Diseases of white blood cells often negatively affect immune function, rendering patients susceptible to severe, potentially life-threatening infections. Disorders of white cells often result in either increased or decreased numbers of the cells, but changes in the shape or size of white cells also occur. Such changes may be indicative of infection. For example, in mononucleosis, lymphocytes are abnormally large, a phenomenon caused by an immune response triggered by infection with Epstein-Barr virus, the cause of the illness.

Diseases of platelets and coagulation underlie various bleeding disorders. These disorders may be characterized by the inability to form a clot to stop bleeding or by excessive clot formation within blood vessels, which can obstruct the flow of blood and lead to a potentially serious adverse cardiovascular event, such as stroke or heart attack. Blood disorders may arise from an inherited genetic mutation or from an acquired defect that causes abnormal platelet activity or clot formation. Examples of bleeding and coagulation disorders include thrombocytopenia, hemophilia, von Willebrand disease, and thrombosis.

DISEASES OF WHITE BLOOD CELLS

Variations in the number of white blood cells occur normally from hour to hour, the highest counts being recorded in the afternoon and the lowest in the early morning. Temporary increases also normally occur during muscular exercise, menstruation, pregnancy, and childbirth, as well as in certain emotional states. Abnormal changes in the count, appearance, or proportion of the various white cells are indicative of pathological conditions in the body.

LEUKOCYTOSIS

Leukocytosis is an abnormally high number of white blood cells (leukocytes) in the blood circulation, defined as more than 10,000 white cells per cubic millimetre of blood. Leukocytosis is most commonly the result of infection. It may also occur after strenuous exercise, convulsions (e.g., epilepsy), emotional stress, anesthesia, the administration of epinephrine, pregnancy and labour, and lack of oxygen (as in the early phases of adaptation to high altitude). Leukocytosis is also observed in certain parasitic

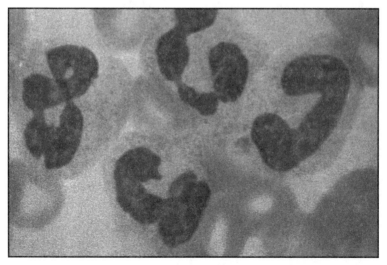

Leukocytosis is characterized by an elevated number of white blood cells (leukocytes) in the blood circulation. Dr. Candler Ballard/Centers for Disease Control and Prevention (CDC) (Image Number: 6048)

infestations, intoxications (metabolic or chemical), chronic diseases (e.g., leukemia), and allergic reactions.

Leukocytosis is usually caused by increased granulocytes (especially neutrophils), some of which may be immature (myelocytes). Most often leukocytosis is the result of the presence of an infection, usually caused by pyogenic (pus-producing) organisms such as *Streptococcus*, *Staphylococcus*, *Gonococcus*, *Pneumococcus*, or *Meningococcus*. White cell counts of 12,000 to 20,000 per cubic millimetre during infections are not unusual. As the number of cells increases, the proportion of immature cells usually rises, perhaps because the demands on the white cell-producing tissues in the bone marrow have increased to the point at which there is an insufficient number of mature cells for delivery into the circulation. As the infection subsides, the number of younger forms and the total white cell count decrease and ultimately return to normal. During the period of repair following an inflammatory reaction, the monocytes may increase in number, and subsequently the lymphocytes will become more numerous.

Certain types of infection are characterized from the beginning by an increase in the number of small lymphocytes unaccompanied by increases in monocytes or granulocytes. Such lymphocytosis is usually of viral origin. Moderate degrees of lymphocytosis are encountered in certain chronic infections such as tuberculosis and brucellosis.

Infectious mononucleosis is associated with the appearance of unusually large lymphocytes (atypical lymphocytes). These cells represent part of the complex defense mechanism against an infectious agent known as Epstein-Barr virus (EBV), and they disappear from the blood when the attack of infectious mononucleosis subsides. Monocytosis, an increase in the number of monocytes in the blood, occurs in association with certain infectious processes, especially subacute bacterial endo-carditis (inflammation of the lining of the heart) and malaria. Monocytosis also occurs when the bone marrow is recovering from a toxic injury.

Eosinophilic leukocytosis, an increase in eosinophilic white cells, is encountered in many allergic reactions and parasitic infections. It is especially characteristic of trichinosis, a disorder resulting from infestation by trichina larvae, which are ingested when poorly cooked infected pork is eaten.

Mononucleosis

Mononucleosis is an infection in humans that is caused by the EBV, and its most common symptoms are fever, general malaise, and sore throat. A condition similar to mononucleosis may be caused by the agents of cytomegalovirus and *Toxoplasma gondii*. The disease occurs predominantly in persons from 10 to 35 years old, but it is known to appear at any age. Infection of young children by EBV usually causes little or no illness, but it does confer immunity against mononucleosis.

Mononucleosis is transmitted primarily by oral contact with exchange of saliva, hence its popular name, "the kissing disease." The incubation period is thought to be about 30 to 40 days. The disease incapacitates individuals for varying periods of time. Some affected people are physically fit for normal activities within two or three weeks, whereas others remain ill for as long as two months.

The symptoms of mononucleosis vary in severity in different persons, but often they are mild. The most common symptoms are fatigue and sore throat. Sometimes the only signs of the disease are fever and generalized discomfort, so the diagnosis is made by study of the blood. The throat is often red, and there is usually a thick, white coating, or membrane, on each tonsil. Swelling of the lymph nodes in the neck, armpits, and groin (for which the disease is sometimes called glandular fever) occurs in some people. Swelling of the upper eyelids is a common finding. In addition, involvement of the liver, as shown by chemical tests, is almost universally present, but severe disease of the liver with jaundice is rare. In about two-thirds of mononucleosis patients, the spleen is enlarged, but death from spleen rupture is infrequent. In rare cases the urine may contain blood.

The blood serum of individuals with mononucleosis contains an antibody (sheep cell or heterophil agglutinin) that is characteristic of the disease, but antibodies against EBV itself are more specific markers of the infection. Thus, changes in the white blood cells and the detection of EBV antibodies in serum are used in the diagnosis of the disease.

Many secondary infections and conditions may arise in a person with mononucleosis. For example, some persons are affected by a rash consisting of multiple small hemorrhages or resembling that of measles or scarlet fever. Pneumonia is present in about 2 percent of the cases. Encephalitis, meningitis, or peripheral neuritis occurs uncommonly.

There is no specific therapy for mononucleosis. Antibiotics are of value only for the secondary bacterial infections (such as bacterial pneumonia) that occur in some cases.

Epstein-Barr Virus

EBV is a virus of the Herpesviridae family that causes acute infectious mononucleosis. The herpesvirus family also includes cytomegalovirus, as well as the viruses that cause cold sores (herpes simplex type 1), genital ulcers (herpes simplex type 2), and shingles (herpes zoster). All these viruses show the property of latency, and in each case immunosuppression can lead to their activation. The most dramatic example of this can be found in AIDS, which causes a pronounced deficiency of T cells (lymphocytes that mature in the thymus). Patients with AIDS can develop severe and even fatal herpesvirus infections.

EBV was first reported by British scientists M.A. Epstein, Y.M. Barr, and B.G. Achong, who found viruslike particles in cells isolated from a newly described lymphatic cancer called Burkitt lymphoma. Later research showed that children can develop antibodies to this virus early in life, evidence that they have been infected with it, without exhibiting any illness and certainly without any signs of tumour growth or of infectious mononucleosis. Mononucleosis thus seems to occur only in those who escaped EBV infection in childhood.

EBV is known to be able to infect only two different types of cells in the body, some salivary gland cells and one special type of white blood cell. Virus that infects the cells of the salivary gland is carried into the mouth in the stream of saliva, which is the only bodily fluid that has been proved to contain infectious EBV particles. White blood cells known as B cells (lymphocytes that are derived in the bone marrow) can also carry EBV. These highly specialized cells manufacture antibodies to help fight infections.

Within the salivary gland the virus growth cycle is completed, and infectious virus particles are generated. Within the B cells, however, the virus growth cycle is abortive, and EBV persists in the B cell in a partially replicated state for the life of the cell. Thus, despite the ability to mount an immune response against EBV, the virus is never completely eliminated from the body. Even though the virus growth in the B cell is incomplete, the lymphocyte is permanently altered by the infectious process (i.e., B cells can take on growth characteristics that resemble those of cancerous lymphocytes). The affected B cells can multiply excessively to produce a cancer of the lymphatic system. In addition, in a normal person carrying latent EBV, if the natural responses of the immune system are suppressed (immunosuppression), the virus can emerge from its latent form and initiate a new round of infection.

In less developed nations, infection with EBV occurs in almost all children younger than age 5 and is not associated with recognizable symptoms. In industrialized nations, about half of the population successfully avoids EBV infection through their late teens or early 20s. When EBV infection is delayed until the teenage or early adult years, the body seems to respond to it differently. In about two-thirds of these cases, infection is asymptomatic or very mild. In the remaining one-third of the cases, infection causes mononucleosis.

Other rare disorders have also been linked with EBV. These include the African lymphoid cancer called Burkitt lymphoma; nasopharyngeal carcinoma, a cancer of the nasal sinuses and throat that is common in southern China, Southeast Asia, and northern Africa and among Eskimos; and certain neurological illnesses, including encephalitis (inflammation of the brain) and paralyses of various nerve groups (for example, Bell palsy, which affects the facial nerve).

There are no specific treatments for any form of EBV infection, and no vaccines have yet been developed.

LEUKOPENIA

Leukopenia is an abnormally low number of white blood cells in the blood circulation, defined as less than 5,000 white cells per cubic millimetre of blood. Leukopenia often accompanies certain infections, especially those caused by viruses or protozoans. Other causes of the condition include the administration of certain drugs (e.g., analgesics, antihistamines, and anticonvulsants), debilitation, malnutrition, chronic anemias, some spleen disorders, agranulocytosis, lupus erythematosus, and anaphylactic shock.

Leukopenia is associated with conditions known as neutropenia and agranulocytosis. In contrast to leukocytosis, which is usually caused by increased neutrophils (neutrophilia), leukopenia usually is caused by a reduction in the number of neutrophils (neutropenia). Of itself, neutropenia causes no symptoms, but people with neutropenia of any cause may have frequent and severe bacterial infections. Agranulocytosis is an acute disorder characterized by severe sore throat, fever, and marked fatigue associated with extreme reduction in the number of neutrophilic granulocytes or even their complete disappearance from the blood.

Neutropenia

Neutropenia may be caused by a hypersensitivity mechanism in which a drug provokes the formation of antibodies. If the drug happens to bind to the neutrophil, the antibody destroys the neutrophil when it reacts with the drug. A second important mechanism of neutropenia is toxic damage to the bone marrow. Chemotherapeutic agents used in the treatment of cancer, particularly leukemia, often produce leukopenia (and neutropenia) by damaging the bone marrow. Other drugs that cause neutropenia include pain relievers (analgesics), antihistamines, tranquilizers, anticonvulsants, antimicrobial agents, sulfonamide derivatives, and antithyroid drugs.

Neutropenia also is associated with certain types of infections (e.g., typhoid, brucellosis, measles, and HIV infection) and with certain diseases involving the bone marrow (e.g., aplastic anemia) or the spleen. In addition, sufficiently high doses of radiation cause neutropenia, as do certain chemotherapeutic agents. Treatment is directed toward the cause of the neutropenia.

Agranulocytosis

Agranulocytosis, also called agranulocytic angina, is an acute infection associated with an extreme reduction of white blood cells (leukopenia), particularly neutrophils (neutropenia). In most cases, agranulocytosis appears to develop as a result of sensitization to certain drugs and chemicals. Infection then follows as a consequence, not a cause, of the profound neutropenia.

First observed as a reaction to the coal-tar product aminopyrine, agranulocytosis is triggered by a variety of pain relievers (analgesics), tranquilizers, antihistamines, anticonvulsants, sulfonamide derivatives, and antithyroid drugs. It also is a frequent complication of cancer treatment. Treatment of agranulocytosis consists of the immediate and permanent withdrawal of the offending drug and control of the infection with antibiotics.

LEUKEMIA

Leukemia is a potentially fatal disease of the blood-forming tissues. The term leukemia means "white blood" and arose from the discovery of extremely large numbers of white blood cells in the blood of certain persons. Counts as high as 500,000 per cubic millimetre and even 1 million per cubic millimetre may be found in some instances. There are two main varieties of leukemia, myelogenous (or granulocytic) and lymphocytic. These terms refer to the types of cell that are involved. Each type is further subdivided into acute and chronic categories, referring to the duration of the untreated disease. Before the advent of modern chemotherapy, patients with acute leukemia usually died within weeks or months of the first manifestations of the disease. The life span of patients with chronic leukemia is now measured in years.

The cause of leukemia is unknown, but researchers have identified certain risk factors that increase a person's chance of developing the disease. Ionizing radiation is a leukemia-inducing agent. Survivors of the atomic bomb explosions in Hiroshima and Nagasaki during World War II, pioneering radiologists who used inadequately shielded apparatus, and certain patients receiving a particular kind of radiation are known to have developed leukemia with a frequency far exceeding that of the general population. Noteworthy is the fact that almost all radiation-induced leukemia has been of the myelogenous variety. The prolonged administration of radiomimetic drugs used in cancer chemotherapy, termed alkylating agents, is also associated with an increased risk of developing leukemia. Some evidence suggests that certain industrial chemicals, notably benzene, may cause leukemia. Genetic factors may lead to an increased frequency of leukemia in certain selected instances. This is suggested by evidence that shows the higher probability for acute leukemia occurring in both identical twins if one is affected as compared with both fraternal twins under the same conditions as well as by the frequency of development of acute myelogenous leukemia in children with Down syndrome, a condition in which there is a recognized chromosome defect.

Advances in molecular genetics have greatly increased the understanding of leukemia. The disease seems to arise from a genetic change (mutation) in an early progenitor, or stem cell, in the bone marrow. The mutant cell passes the genetic change on to all of its progeny, thus giving rise to a clone of leukemic cells. In many cases of leukemia, the mutation is detectable by analysis of the chromosomes of leukemic cells. A well-studied abnormality of this type, the Philadelphia chromosome, occurs in almost all cases of chronic myelogenous leukemia. The chromosomal aberrations affect genes that influence vital aspects of cell growth and function. These genes, the oncogenes, may themselves be mutated or their regulation may be abnormal. The entire process, beginning with the mutation, usually involves many steps that culminate in a cell with the malignant attributes of a leukemic cell. This concept of the mechanism of leukemia has influenced treatment of the disease, which aims to eliminate the mutant clone and all of its progeny by chemotherapy or bone marrow transplantation.

Leukemia primarily involves the bone marrow, but the lymph nodes and spleen may also be affected. Changes also take place in the white cells, red blood cells, and platelets, with consequent anemia and bleeding manifestations. There may be weakness and an increased tendency to

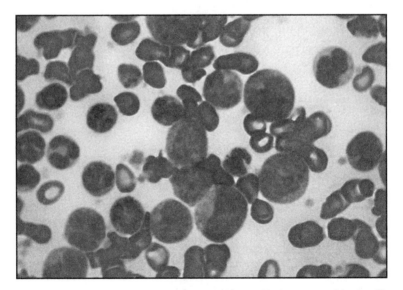

A blood slide revealing abnormalities in blast cells (immature blood cells) that are symptomatic of myelogenus leukemia. The disease is believed to start as a genetic mutation in bone marrow stem cells. CDC/ Stacy Howard

become fatigued because of anemia, in addition to hemor-rhages into the skin, nosebleeds, or gum bleeding caused by a decrease in the number of platelets. Leukemia is diag-nosed by examination of the blood, supplemented in most instances by examination of the bone marrow.

Acute leukemia is marked by the presence in the blood of immature cells normally not present. In acute lympho-cytic anemia (ALL), most frequently seen in children, the cells are immature forms of the lymphatic series of cells. In acute myelogenous leukemia (AML), the predominant cells are the youngest recognizable precursors (myelo-blasts) of the neutrophils of the blood. In a third and the least common variety, acute monocytic leukemia, the immature cells appear to be precursors of the monocytes of the blood. Myelogenous and monocytic leukemia occur more commonly in adults and adolescents than in young children. In general, acute leukemia occurs in young per-sons, but no age group is exempt. The total white cell count usually is increased but commonly is normal or lower than normal (leukopenic). In such cases abnormal immature cells may nevertheless be seen in the blood. In all forms of acute leukemia, the typical cells are found in abundance in the bone marrow.

Chronic myelogenous leukemia (CML) is character-ized by the appearance in the blood of large numbers of immature white blood cells of the myelogenous series in the stage following the myeloblast, namely, myelocytes. The spleen becomes enlarged, anemia develops, and the affected person may lose weight. The platelets may be normal or increased in number, abnormally low values being found only in the late stages of the disease or as an unintended result of therapy. The disease is most com-monly encountered in persons between ages 30 and 60.

With treatment the white cell count falls to normal, anemia is relieved, and the size of the spleen is greatly reduced. When the white cell count rises again, treatment is reinstituted. Such cycles of treatment, remission, and relapse with rise of white cell count can be repeated many times, but a stage ultimately is reached when treatment is ineffective. The disease then often terminates in a form resembling acute leukemia (blastic crisis). There is considerable variation in the duration of the disease. Although in various series the average life span has been about 3 years, many affected persons live in good general condition for 5 to 10 years and sometimes longer.

Chronic lymphocytic leukemia (CLL) differs in many ways from other forms of leukemia. It occurs most often in people older than 50 years of age, and its course usually is rather benign. It is mainly characterized by an increase in the number of lymphocytes in the blood, often accompanied by more or less generalized enlargement of lymph nodes and the spleen. Affected persons may go for many years without treatment and without any other manifestations. There may be no anemia and no weight loss. Life span in this disease is measured in terms of 5 to 15 years, occasionally even longer. Two events mark a change in the state of relative good health. One is the development of anemia, sometimes hemolytic in type, often accompanied by some decrease in the number of platelets. The other is impairment of immune mechanisms, resulting in great susceptibility to bacterial infections.

Treatment differs according to the type of leukemia. Consequently, proper classification of the leukemia is the first step, once the diagnosis of leukemia has been made. A number of drugs are used for the treatment of leukemia, and, while now less frequently than before chemotherapy was available, so are various forms of radiation. The therapeutic agents are all myelotoxic (i.e., they injure all the cells of the bone marrow, normal cells as well as leukemic cells). Their mode of action is through direct damage to

the dividing stem cell (unspecialized cell from which specialized cells develop) or by slowing or cessation of cell
division (mitosis). These effects may be accomplished by
antimetabolites, drugs that interfere with the synthesis of
DNA, a constituent of the chromosomes in the cell
nucleus; blocking DNA strand duplication by binding
drugs such as nitrogen mustard with the base groups of
DNA; disruption of the mitotic spindle during mitosis; or
interfering with the formation or functioning of ribonucleic acid (RNA), which is manufactured in the cell nucleus
and plays an essential role in the production of protein
and in other cell functions. Drugs with different modes of
action are often combined, especially in the treatment of
acute leukemia. In the process of treatment, anemia may
increase. The body's defenses, through the decrease in the
number of neutrophils, may be impaired, and the platelets
may be greatly reduced in number. Anemia can be treated
with blood transfusions, and serious reductions in platelets can be met for a time with platelet transfusions.

Acute lymphocytic leukemia is more successfully
treated than are other forms of acute leukemia. Prolonged
remissions and even cures can be brought about in children with the disease. Certain drugs are used to bring
about remission. If the remission is complete, the patient
becomes well, and no signs of the disease are demonstra-
ble in the blood or bone marrow. Drugs other than those
used to induce remission often are more useful in maintaining the remission than the remission-inducing drugs.

Acute myelogenous leukemia and acute monocytic leukemia are less effectively treated by available drugs than is
acute lymphocytic leukemia. Nevertheless, new and
aggressive forms of chemotherapy can induce lengthy
remissions of the disease. Transplantation of normal bone
marrow, often from histocompatible siblings, following

total radiation of the patient to destroy all normal bone marrow cells as well as the leukemic cells, has shown promise. Although the treatment is arduous and complex, cures of acute lymphocytic and acute myelogenous forms of leukemia are possible with bone marrow transplantation.

Chronic myelogenous leukemia is treated with the drugs hydroxyurea or busulfan in daily doses until the white cell count has returned to normal. Treatment then is interrupted until the white cell count has risen to about 50,000 cells per cubic millimetre, when treatment is resumed. This can be repeated many times, and thus the affected person is maintained in good health for years. Frequently, the intervals between treatments are six months or longer. Busulfan, however, like other antileukemic agents, can injure the bone marrow, and other adverse effects may occur. Other drugs and radiation therapy also have been used but are somewhat less valuable than hydroxyurea or busulfan. In suitable young patients, bone marrow transplantation has been successful in chronic myelogenous leukemia.

In its early stages, chronic lymphocytic leukemia seems best untreated, as long as anemia is not present or glandular enlargement is not too troublesome. None of the current treatments are curative. The high white cell counts in themselves are not harmful. When there is severe anemia, however, or when the platelet count is very low and bleeding manifestations are severe, adrenocorticosteroid hormones are often given.

LYMPHOMA

Lymphoma is characterized by malignant tumours of lymphocytes that are usually not associated with a leukemic blood picture. Instead, enlargement of lymph nodes, the spleen, or both are characteristic. The lymphomas are classified into two main groups: Hodgkin disease and non-Hodgkin lymphoma (or lymphocytic lymphoma). Hodgkin disease usually begins with a painless swelling of a lymph node, and it may involve lymph nodes anywhere in the body. Non-Hodgkin lymphoma arises from either B cells or T cells. It may have an indolent course, as in the nodular well-differentiated B cell lymphomas, or the tumour may be aggressive, as in the diffuse T cell forms. Unlike Hodgkin disease, non-Hodgkin lymphoma spreads through the bloodstream.

Viruses have been shown to cause lymphoma in mice, rats, cats, and cows. These animal viruses are not infectious for human cells. A human retrovirus, human T-cell lymphotropic virus (HTLV-I), has been suggested to be the cause of a type of lymphoma called T-cell lymphoma. Cases of T-cell lymphoma associated with HTLV-I have been found in clusters in southern Japan (Kyushu) and in the coastal region of Georgia in the United States, but sporadic cases also have been identified.

The disease seems to begin in one lymph node and spread to others. Exact determination of the extent of Hodgkin disease (staging) is important in planning its treatment. This entails a thorough medical examination, a bone marrow biopsy, and X-rays. The latter usually include computerized axial tomography (CAT) scanning to identify enlarged lymph nodes in the interior of the body. In many cases, surgery (laparotomy) is required to obtain for examination lymph nodes from deep within the abdomen. The early stages of Hodgkin disease can be cured with radiation therapy. More advanced stages are still curable with chemotherapy, and in some patients a combination of chemotherapy and radiation therapy is used.

In non-Hodgkin lymphoma, the staging procedure is not as extensive as in Hodgkin disease. Combination chemotherapy, usually given in cycles over a period of months, is effective in certain types of non-Hodgkin lymphoma. Prolonged remission with eradication of the disease is difficult to achieve in the indolent nodular lymphomas.

MULTIPLE MYELOMA

Multiple myeloma, also called plasma cell myeloma (or myelomatosis), is a malignant proliferation of cells within the bone marrow that usually occurs during middle age or later and increases in occurrence with age. Myelomas are equally common in males and females and affect any of the marrow-containing bones such as the skull, flat bones (e.g., ribs, sternum, pelvis, shoulder blades), and vertebrae.

The disease manifests as a proliferation of abnormal plasma cells or plasmablasts that populate the bone marrow throughout the body. The plasma cells are the progeny of a single malignant clone and secrete into the blood a single type of immunoglobulin molecule, a monoclonal antibody. The monoclonal antibodies can replace the normal antibodies in the blood, thereby reducing the ability of the body to ward off infection. In some cases, a component of immunoglobulin, the light chain, may be produced in excess. These light chains appear in the urine, and in multiple myeloma they are called Bence Jones proteins. A type of chronic kidney disease often develops, probably as a result of the high concentration of Bence Jones proteins in the kidney tubules. Frequently, this is the ultimate cause of death. In addition, bone destruction that releases calcium into the circulation may result in calcium deposition in the kidneys and other abnormal sites.

Multiple myeloma is a severely painful disorder and causes defects in the bone of the skull, ribs, spine, and pelvis that ultimately result in fractures. As the bone marrow becomes more involved, anemia develops and hemorrhages occur. The number of white blood cells may be low, and abnormal myeloma or plasma cells are found in the bone marrow. Thus, symptoms and signs of multiple myeloma include pain, anemia, weakness, susceptibility to infection, a tendency to hemorrhage, shortness of breath, and kidney insufficiency. In addition, pathological bone fractures may occur in the vertebrae, giving rise to neurological symptoms.

The disease is progressive and is considered incurable. Current treatments are directed toward changing multiple myeloma into a manageable chronic disease and increasing the overall survival rate. Drugs commonly used for the treatment of the disease include adrenocorticosteroid hormones and chemotherapeutic agents. Thalidomide is often used initially to treat multiple myeloma and can prevent progression for a variable length of time. When appropriate, bone-marrow transplantation after high-dose chemotherapy can lead to long-term survival. However, the success rate is variable, with complete remissions lasting from only a few months to many years. In the rare instances that a malignant proliferation of plasma cells is confined to one location, the tumour is called a plasmacytoma and can be treated with irradiation or surgery.

BLEEDING DISORDERS

Bleeding disorders may result from inherited or acquired defects of clotting or platelet function. The usual consequence is persistent bleeding from injuries that would normally cause little trouble. Some persons may bleed more easily than normal, perhaps even spontaneously, as a result of an increased fragility of the blood vessels. This fragility is not a hemostatic defect but may be associated with one. The most characteristic feature of blood clotting defects, as typified by hemophilia, are recurrent, crippling hemorrhages into joints and muscles and bleeding into body cavities. Platelet abnormalities are associated with spontaneous bleeding from the membranes of the nose, mouth, and gastrointestinal and urogenital tracts.

The diagnosis of hemostatic defects depends on clinical and laboratory data. Investigation of the affected person's family history is important because many of these conditions are inherited. The personal history reveals the type of bleeding and the possible effects of drugs, chemicals, allergy, infection, or dietary abnormalities. Physical examination reveals visible hemorrhages or vascular lesions and the effects of internal bleeding. Platelets are evaluated by counting them; examining their appearance; and testing functions such as the bleeding time, platelet adhesiveness, and platelet aggregation. Tests of clotting function include such indicators as the prothrombin time and the partial thromboplastin time. These tests allow a deficiency of any of the clotting factors to be identified and a quantitative assessment of activity of individual factors to be made. Most cases of abnormal bleeding can thus be traced to specific defects. Precise diagnosis often permits specific and effective treatment. General treatment of bleeding disorders consists mainly of temporary replacement therapy by transfusion.

THROMBOCYTOPENIA

Thrombocytopenia is an abnormally low number of platelets (thrombocytes) in the circulation. Normal platelet counts are between 150,000 and 400,000 per cubic millimetre. When the platelet count drops to 50,000 to 75,000 per cubic millimetre, and particularly to 10,000 to 20,000 per cubic millimetre, spontaneous bleeding may occur.

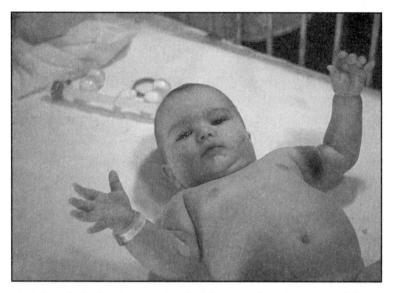

An infant displaying the spotted rash and deep bruising indicative of throm-bocytopenia. The condition is marked by a drop in the number of platelets necessary for clotting. California Department of Public Health

Thrombocytopenia is associated with blood diseases such as aplastic anemia and leukemia and is attributed to impaired production of platelets. Similarly, excessive radiation, exposure to certain chemicals (such as benzene), or drugs used in cancer chemotherapy decrease the production of platelets. In sensitive persons, drugs such as quinidine (used in the treatment of malaria) provoke platelet antibodies and platelet destruction, resulting in thrombocytopenia. Other causes of thrombocytopenia include a congenital lack of megakaryocytes (cells in the bone marrow that give rise to platelets) and increased platelet destruction (e.g., from a malfunctioning spleen, congestive heart failure, blood transfusion after hemorrhage, or incompatible blood transfusion). Thrombocytopenia also may accompany certain infections such as measles and autoimmune disorders such as systemic lupus erythematosus and idiopathic thrombocytopenic purpura.

Thrombocytopenia is characterized by the appearance of tiny purplish spots (petechiae) or larger black-and-blue areas (ecchymoses) in the skin, which are caused by small hemorrhages into the skin. Other symptoms include nosebleeds and easy bruising, and sometimes gastrointestinal bleeding, excess menstrual bleeding, or other hemorrhage is observed. Hemorrhage in the brain can have serious consequences. Treatment includes rest, protection from injury, and sometimes platelet transfusion.

DISORDERS OF PLATELET FUNCTION

Some bleeding disorders are caused by abnormalities of platelet function rather than to a defect in platelet number. Glanzmann thrombasthenia, an inherited disorder associated with a mild bleeding tendency, is the result of a deficiency of the platelet glycoprotein IIb–IIIa, which is required for normal platelet function. Bernard-Soulier syndrome, an inherited disorder associated with a pronounced bleeding tendency, is caused by a deficiency of glycoprotein Ib, also necessary for normal platelet function, on the platelet membrane. The platelets in this disease are unusually large. Many other platelet defects exist, but they have not been fully characterized at a biochemical level.

The most common acquired disorder of platelet function is associated with aspirin, or acetylsalicylic acid. Aspirin reacts with platelets, even when the drug is taken at low doses. This reaction impairs the ability of platelets to produce a group of chemicals known as prostaglandins, which stimulate inflammation. The inhibition of prostaglandin biosynthesis and the decrease in the production of thromboxane A$_2$, a substance secreted by platelets that diminishes blood loss, can be associated with a bleeding disorder. Other drugs have a similar effect, but aspirin is especially important because of its wide use and the sensitivity of certain persons to its action.

VASCULAR CAUSES OF BLEEDING DISORDERS

Vascular defects causing abnormal bleeding are rare. In cases of vitamin C deficiency (scurvy), capillary integrity is lost, and blood seeps into the tissues. In the inherited condition hemorrhagic telangiectasia, groups of enormously dilated capillaries can be seen in the skin and mucous membranes of the mouth, nose, and gastrointestinal and respiratory tracts. The lesions appear in adult life and tend to bleed on the least provocation. Ehlers-Danlos syndrome is a disorder of collagen synthesis in which the increased fragility of vessels causes them to be easily ruptured. The use of cortisone, prednisolone, and other glucocorticoid drugs are associated with increased capillary fragility and purpura (pinpoint hemorrhages in the skin and mucous membranes).

COAGULATION DISORDERS

Coagulation disorders include a number of disorders that are related to defects in the clotting of blood. Deficiencies in any of the protein factors involved in coagulation can result in hemorrhages following minor injuries. In some of these disorders, a specific deficiency is the result of an inherited defect (e.g., hemophilia). In others an acquired pathological condition may be responsible for the deficiency (e.g., conditions interfering with absorption of vitamin K and severe infection).

Two examples of the diverse causes of coagulation disorders are afibrinogenemia, or hypofibrinogenemia, and disseminated intravascular coagulation. Afibrinogenemia refers to a reduction in the amount of the clotting factor fibrinogen in the blood. This is seen in rare instances as an inherited disorder, but more commonly it is found as part of the syndrome of disseminated intravascular coagulation. The latter is an acquired disorder in which platelets and blood-clotting components are consumed until a severe deficiency exists, resulting in a bleeding disorder. In addition, the fibrinolytic system (the system that dissolves clots) is also activated, leading to the destruction of fibrinogen and fibrin clots. Numerous primary problems can be responsible for this activation: bacteria and bacterial products, dead or injured cells as a result of tissue injury or surgery, cells from the placenta or a dead fetus, certain forms of cancer, and venom from snakebites.

The clotting deficiencies are treated with plasma or plasma proteins containing the missing factor. These agents can restore hemostatic function to normal for hours or days and, with continued treatment, allow injuries to heal or complicated surgery to be performed. In some cases, such as disseminated intravascular coagulation, treatment may involve the removal of the inciting cause of the activation of the blood coagulation system.

Hemophilia

The best-known coagulation disorder is hemophilia, which is caused by an inherited defect transmitted by the female but manifested almost exclusively in the male. The most common form of hemophilia, hemophilia A, is caused by the absence of the coagulation protein factor VIII (antihemophilic globulin). Approximately 85 percent of persons with hemophilia have factor VIII deficiency. The next most common form of hemophilia, hemophilia B, is the result of deficiency of factor IX (plasma thromboplastin component, or PTC). Both factor VIII deficiency and factor IX deficiency have signs and symptoms that are indistinguishable. Spontaneous bleeding into joints, giving rise to severe chronic arthritis, is a common problem among persons with severe hemophilia. Additionally, there is bleeding into the brain and the abdominal cavity, as well as marked bruising. In general, the greater the deficiency in either factor VIII or factor IX, the more severe the manifestations of disease.

Treatment of bleeding episodes emphasizes the replacement of the missing plasma protein. In a patient with hemophilia A, factor VIII can be replaced by the infusion into a vein of plasma derived from a normal donor, the cryoprecipitate fraction of normal plasma, or a partially purified preparation of factor VIII derived from normal plasma. The peptide desmopressin (DDAVP) helps treat milder forms of hemophilia A. Similarly, in a patient with hemophilia B, factor IX can be replaced by the infusion into the vein of plasma derived from a normal donor or a partially purified preparation of factor IX derived from normal plasma. New methods of preparing factor VIII and factor IX, using genetic engineering techniques, have led to the introduction of safer factor VIII and factor IX generated by recombinant DNA methods. With the current methods of medical care, persons with hemophilia can live nearly normal, productive lives. Major surgery, if needed, can be accomplished by administering the missing protein.

VITAMIN K DEFICIENCY

Vitamin K deficiency leads to a deficit of the proteins that require vitamin K for their synthesis, including pro-thrombin, factor X, factor IX, and factor VII. Vitamin K deficiency is associated with obstructive jaundice, in which the flow of bile into the bowel is interrupted. Bile is necessary for the absorption of vitamin K. Similar changes may take place when absorption of vitamin K is impaired by conditions such as chronic diarrhea or with the administration of certain antibiotics. Vitamin K deficiency also occurs in the newborn infant as hemorrhagic disease of the newborn. This form of pro-thrombin deficiency can be prevented by administration of vitamin K to the baby shortly after birth. Accidental consumption or overdoses of the anticoagulant drug warfarin can lead to a deficiency of the vitamin K-dependent blood-clotting proteins and a serious bleeding tendency.

VON WILLEBRAND DISEASE

Von Willebrand disease is an inherited blood disorder characterized by a prolonged bleeding time and a deficiency of factor VIII, an important blood-clotting agent. This disorder is caused by deficiencies in von Willebrand factor (VWF), a molecule that facilitates platelet adhesion and is a plasma carrier for factor VIII. Symptoms usually include abnormal bruising, bleeding from mucosal surfaces such as the gums and the gastrointestinal tract, and prolonged bleeding from any break in the skin or during surgery. The level of VWF and the severity of the disease vary over time, often as a result of hormonal or immune responses.

Von Willebrand disease types 1 and 2 are milder forms and are inherited as autosomal dominant traits. Type 3, the most severe form, is recessive and requires that the trait be inherited from both parents. The disease is treated with desmopressin (DDAVP), a drug that increases levels of factor VIII and VWF, or plasma-derived factor VIII preparations.

Von Willebrand Factor

A glycoprotein that plays an important role in stopping the escape of blood from vessels (hemostasis) following vascular injury, VWF works by mediating the adherence of platelets to one another and to sites of vascular damage. VWF binds to a protein complex made up of the glycoproteins Ib, IX, and V on the surfaces of platelets. Binding VWF to this complex facilitates the activation and aggregation of platelets and the interaction of platelets with components such as collagen in the damaged vessel lining. These actions are important in the formation of a blood clot that halts bleeding.

VWF circulates in low concentrations in the plasma portion of blood and is made by cells in the bone marrow and by endothelial cells, which form the lining on the inside surface of blood vessels. The protein is activated by flowing blood and thus has the potential to stimulate the formation of blood clots even in the absence of vessel damage. To prevent unnecessary clotting, VWF is regulated by an enzyme known as ADAMTS13. When VWF is active, it exists in an unfolded form, which exposes its platelet-binding domains and thus allows it to bind to the glycoprotein complexes on platelets. However, unfolding also exposes cleavage sites for ADAMTS13, which cuts VWF into fragments that have little or no ability to bind to and activate platelets.

There are more than 300 mutations in the *VWF* gene that can cause von Willebrand disease, in which reduced or delayed clot formation results in prolonged bleeding following vascular injury. Some mutations are associated with only slightly reduced levels or activity of VWF, whereas others are associated with drastic reductions leading to severe disease. In contrast, mutations that affect ADAMTS13 cause diseases characterized by excess clotting and have been associated with familial thrombotic thrombocytopenic purpura, a rare disorder involving abnormal blood coagulation.

Thrombocytopathy

Thrombocytopathies are any of several blood disorders characterized by dysfunctional platelets (thrombocytes), which result in prolonged bleeding time, defective clot formation, and a tendency to hemorrhage. Inherited thrombocytopathies include von Willebrand disease; thrombasthenia, characterized by abnormal clot retraction and defective platelet aggregation; and Bernard-Soulier syndrome, characterized by unusually large platelets. In addition, thrombocytopathy is sometimes seen in cases of Down syndrome and Wiskott-Aldrich syndrome (an immune disorder).

Acquired thrombocytopathy has been known to be associated with several disorders, including cirrhosis, leukemia, pernicious anemia, scurvy, and uremia. Temporary platelet dysfunction is sometimes induced by such drugs as antihistamines, aspirin, indomethacin, phenothiazines, phenylbutazone, and tricyclic antidepressants.

Treatment for congenital thrombocytopathy is platelet transfusion to control bleeding. For acquired thrombocytopathies, cure of the underlying disease usually results in improved platelet function.

THROMBOSIS

Thrombosis, the formation of a blood clot (thrombus) that tends to plug functionally normal blood vessels, is one of the major causes of death in Western societies. In this condition the normal tendency of platelets to form a clot at the site of a vascular injury is a contributing factor. The process of thrombosis is not completely understood, but the chief underlying cause is believed to be a lesion (atherosclerosis) that destroys the normal endothelial surface of the blood vessel. Platelets tend to adhere to such lesions and eventually form masses that, when reinforced by fibrin, may completely obstruct the blood flow. This obstruction may have disastrous consequences in arteries such as the coronary or cerebral blood vessels or a major artery of a limb or organ. In veins the local results are less apparent or perhaps not even detected. Behind the original thrombus, however, the whole blood content of the vein may clot to form a large mass. This occurs most frequently in the leg veins and may be caused by slowing blood flow during a prolonged surgical procedure or confinement to bed. The danger is that the thrombus may become detached (an embolus) and be swept into the pulmonary artery, causing circulatory obstruction in the lung.

The hereditary deficiency of antithrombin III, protein C, protein S, and plasminogen can be associated with a thrombotic tendency (i.e., the inappropriate formation of clots in vessels). The most common thrombotic disorders include pulmonary embolism (clots in the lung) and deep vein thrombosis (formation of clots in the leg veins). Other predisposing causes of thrombosis are increased platelet numbers in the blood and the formation of functionally abnormal platelets in diseases of the bone marrow. The use of birth control pills, pregnancy, and many disorders may be associated with a thrombotic tendency, but the reasons for this association are unclear.

The prevention and treatment of thrombosis aims at balancing the overactive clotting tendency and a bleeding tendency. The formation of clots may be prevented by the administration of anticoagulant drugs. Warfarin inhibits the action of vitamin K and renders the blood less able to clot. Heparin facilitates the inhibition of activated clotting enzymes with the inhibitor, antithrombin III. These commonly used medications prevent the formation of clots or the enlargement of already existing clots. Streptokinase, urokinase, and tissue plasminogen activator are enzymes that are used therapeutically to dissolve clots. As agents that cause the lysis of fibrin clots, they are known collectively as fibrinolytic agents. Their administration, although attended by the possibility of bleeding complications, can restore blood flow through a vessel blocked by a clot.

CONCLUSION

The modern understanding of blood, including the details of its various components and knowledge of its life-supporting properties, is the result of centuries of scientific study and investigation. Today, scientists continue to investigate the constituents of blood, attempting to identify substances that can serve as biomarkers, which are detectable and measurable indicators of disease. One approach to identifying blood biomarkers involves systematically characterizing all the proteins known to occur in the blood. This process, though tedious and difficult, promises to reveal a wealth of information about blood proteins, potentially uncovering new details about the role these substances play in health and disease.

Another important area of blood research involves the generation of artificial blood, or blood substitutes, which have potential applications in blood transfusion and organ preservation. One of the greatest challenges confronting the development of these products is their capability of carrying oxygen in quantities sufficient to support the oxygen demands of tissues. Blood substitutes also must be devoid of substances that elicit immune responses once inside the body. If these obstacles can be overcome, blood substitutes could significantly decrease the risks associated with blood transfusion. They also could substantially increase the supply of blood products available for transfusion, which is currently limited by the necessity of donation.

Appendix: Tables

THE ABO AND RH GROUPS IN TRANSFUSION			
SYSTEM	**RECIPIENT TYPE**	**DONOR RED CELL TYPE**	**DONOR PLASMA TYPE**
ABO	A	A* or O	A or AB
ABO	B	B or O	B or AB
ABO	O	O only	O, A, B, or AB
ABO	AB	AB*, A*, B, or O	AB
Rh	positive	positive or negative	positive or negative
Rh	negative	negative or positive**, ***	negative or positive**

*Not if the patient's serum contains anti-A1 (antibody to common type A red cell in subgroup A patients).

**Not if the patient is a female less than 45 years old (childbearing possible), unless life-threatening hemorrhage is present and transfusion of Rh-positive blood is lifesaving.

***Not if the patient's serum contains anti-D (antibody to positive red cells), except under unusual medical circumstances.

REFERENCE VALUES IN HEMATOLOGY*

COMPONENT	SI UNITS	CONVENTIONAL UNITS
red blood cell count		
female	$4.2–5.4 \times 10^{12}/l$	$4.2–5.4 \times 10^6/mm^3$
male	$4.6–6.2 \times 10^{12}/l$	$4.6–6.2 \times 10^6/mm^3$
white blood cell count	$4.5–11.0 \times 10^9/l$	$4,500–11,000/mm^3$
differential white blood cell count		
band neutrophils	$150–400/mm^3$	3–5%
segmented neutrophils	$3,000–5,800/mm^3$	54–62%
lymphocytes	$1,500–3,000/mm^3$	25–33%
monocytes	$300–500/mm^3$	3–7%
eosinophils	$50–250/mm^3$	1–3%
basophils	$15–50/mm^3$	0–1%
hemoglobin		
female	120–160 g/l	12.0–16.0 g/dl
male	130–180 g/l	13.0–18.0 g/dl
hematocrit		
female	0.37–0.47	37–47%
male	0.40–0.54	40–54%
mean corpuscular volume	80–96 femtolitres	$80–96 \, \mu m^3$
reticulocyte count	$25–75 \times 10^9/l$	$25,000–75,000/mm^3$
platelet count	$150–350 \times 10^9/l$	$150–350 \times 10^3/mm^3$
prothrombin time	12–14 seconds	12–14 seconds
partial thromboplastin time	20–35 seconds	20–35 seconds
plasma fibrinogen	2.0–4.0 g/l	200–400 mg/dl
erythrocyte sedimentation rate		
female	0–20 mm/h	0–20 mm/h
male	0–15 mm/h	0–15 mm/h

*All values given for adults.

GLOSSARY

agglutination test Basic technique in identification of the antigens and antibodies of blood groups.

anemia Condition in which the red blood cells (erythrocytes) are reduced in number or volume or are deficient in hemoglobin, their oxygen-carrying pigment.

antiserum Blood serum that contains specific antibodies against an infective organism or poisonous substance.

Bohr effect The effect of pH on the ability of hemoglobin to bind oxygen. When pH is low, hemoglobin binds oxygen less strongly, and when pH is high (as in the lungs), hemoglobin binds more tightly to oxygen.

coagulation The replacement of a relatively unstable platelet plug with a stronger, more resilient blood clot through a series of interdependent, enzyme-mediated reactions.

complement In immunology, a complex system of more than 30 proteins that act in concert to help eliminate infectious microorganisms.

cytokines Any of a group of small, short-lived proteins that are released by one cell to regulate the function of another cell, thereby serving as intercellular chemical messengers.

diastolic pressure Residual pressure exerted on the arteries as the heart relaxes between beats; the lower pressure and the second number recorded when taking blood pressure.

erythropoiesis The process of red cell production.

fibrin A protein that is generated in response to bleeding and that is insoluble; the major component of the blood clot.

globulins Heterogeneous array of proteins of widely varying structure and function.

glycoprotein A substance that is made up of a carbohydrate plus a protein..

hematopoiesis The continuous process by which the cellular constituents of blood are replenished as needed, also known as blood cell formation.

hemoglobin Iron-containing protein found in the red blood cells that transports oxygen to the tissues.

hemolysis The breakdown or destruction of red blood cells so that the contained hemoglobin is freed into the surrounding medium.

hemophilia A hereditary bleeding disorder caused by a deficiency of a substance necessary for blood clotting (coagulation).

hemostasis The prevention of loss of blood from damaged blood vessels by formation of a clot.

immunogenic Capable of inducing antibody formation.

immunoglobulins A class of proteins secreted by cells of the immune system that provide most of the body's supply of protective antibodies.

leukocytosis An abnormally high number of white blood cells (leukocytes) in the blood circulation, defined as more than 10,000 white cells per cubic millimetre of blood.

leukopenia An abnormally low number of white blood cells in the blood circulation, defined as less than 5,000 white cells per cubic millimetre of blood.

lipid Any of a diverse group of organic compounds that are grouped together because they do not interact appreciably with water.

mitosis A process of cell duplication, or reproduction, during which one cell gives rise to two genetically identical daughter cells.

oncogene Genetic material that carries the ability to induce cancer.

polycythemia An abnormal increase in red blood cells and hemoglobin in the circulation, which results in thickened blood, retarded flow, and an increased danger of clot formation.

porphyrins Water-soluble, nitrogenous biological pigments (biochromes), derivatives of which include the hemoproteins (porphyrins combined with metals and protein).

serum The portion of plasma remaining after coagulation of blood.

serum albumin Protein found in blood plasma that helps maintain the osmotic pressure between the blood vessels and tissues.

stem cell An undifferentiated cell that can divide to produce some offspring cells that are destined to differentiate.

systolic pressure The force that blood exerts on the artery walls as the heart contracts to pump the blood to the peripheral organs and tissues; the higher pressure and the first number recorded when taking blood pressure.

thrombocytopenia An abnormally low number of platelets (thrombocytes) in the circulation.

thromboplastin A protein that is present in tissues, platelets, and white blood cells and is required for the coagulation of blood.

thrombosis The formation of a blood clot in the heart or in a blood vessel.

BIBLIOGRAPHY

Further information on human blood is found in the textbooks Marshall A. Lichtman et al. (eds.), *Williams Hematology,* 7th ed. (2006); and Ronald Hoffman et al. (eds.), *Hematology: Basic Principles and Practice,* 4th ed. (2004). Shauna C. Anderson and Keila Poulsen (eds.), *Atlas of Hematology* (2003), offers a complete set of colour photomicrographs of blood cells and is a print companion to two CD-ROMs: *Anderson's Electronic Atlas of Hematology,* 2nd ed. (2002), and *Anderson's Electronic Atlas of Hematologic Disorders* (2003). The biochemical mechanisms involved in bleeding and blood clotting are covered in Robert W. Colman et al. (eds.), *Hemostasis and Thrombosis: Basic Principles and Clinical Practice*, 5th ed. (2005).

Major texts dealing with diseases of the blood include George Stamatoyannopoulos et al. (eds.), *The Molecular Basis of Blood Diseases*, 3rd ed. (2000); I. Chanarin, *The Megaloblastic Anaemias*, 3rd ed. (1990), a comprehensive work with numerous references; D.J. Weatherall, *The Thalassaemia Syndromes*, 4th ed. (2001); Edward S. Henderson and T. Andrew Lister (eds.), *William Dameshek and Frederick Gunz's Leukemia*, 5th ed. (1990); Oscar D. Ratnoff and Charles D. Forbes (ed.), *Disorders of Hemostasis*, 2nd ed. (1991); and Sheila T. Callender, *Blood Disorders: The Facts* (1985), a comprehensive basic introduction.

Additional information on anemia and related diseases of the blood can be found in Kenneth Bridges and Howard A. Pearson, *Anemias and Other Red Cell Disorders* (2008). Blood cancers, including leukemia and lymphoma, are discussed in detail in Peter H. Wiernik et al. (eds.), *Neoplastic Diseases of the Blood* (2003).

Bone marrow and the diseases that affect this tissue are covered in Barbara J. Bain, David M. Clark, and Bridget S. Wilkins, *Bone Marrow Pathology*, 3rd ed. (2001). Approaches to bone marrow transplantation, as well as associated complications are addressed in Joseph H. Antin MD and Deborah S. Yolin, *Manual of Stem Cell and Bone Marrow Transplantation* (2009).

An introduction to blood groups, with information on the major groups and on approaches to blood typing, is Geoff Daniels and Imelda Bromilow, *Essential Guide to Blood Groups* (2007). Information on the different types of blood cells, enhanced by detailed images, is provided in Gene Gulati and Jaime Caro, *Blood Cells: An Atlas of Morphology with Clinical Relevance* (2007). The components and function of blood plasma are discussed in Johann Schaller et al., *Human Blood Plasma Proteins: Structure and Function* (2008).

An introduction to the laboratory analysis of blood is provided in Barbara J. Bain, *Blood Cells: A Practical Guide,* 4th ed. (2006).

INDEX

A

acanthocytosis, 35, 103
Achong, B.G., 202
African Americans, 98, 103, 105, 106, 109, 179
Africans, 38, 101, 105, 110, 119, 182, 185, 186, 203
AIDS, 130, 147, 202
albumin
  carrier protein, 25, 127
  osmotic effect, 23, 24, 127, 128
aldosterone, 27, 28
allergies, 25, 41, 42, 45, 49, 131, 144, 149, 199, 200, 215
altitude, 35, 57, 58, 131, 191, 198
anemia, 56, 57, 58, 131, 133, 138, 142, 143, 144, 159, 161, 162, 163–193, 207–208, 210, 211, 214
  aplastic, 157, 164, 172–174, 204
  fetal, 96
  hemolytic, 34, 109, 133, 136–137, 166, 177–181, 209
  iron deficiency, 124, 134, 164, 174, 175–177
  pernicious, 35, 164, 167, 168, 169–170, 223
  sickle cell, 35, 38, 157, 164, 182, 183, 186–190
animals lacking blood, 19–20
antigen-presenting cells, 42, 47, 50

apheresis, 143, 160
Asians, 97, 106, 110, 119, 182, 203
aspirin, 131, 217–218, 223
Auberger antigens, 102
Australian Aborigines, 119

B

Barr, Y.M., 202
basophils, 41–42, 46–47, 131
B cells, 48–50, 202–203, 212
Bedouins, 101
Bernard-Soulier syndrome, 217, 223
bile, 60, 67, 72, 124, 221
bilirubin, 25, 35, 60, 72, 124, 177
Blackfoot Indians, 97, 119
blood bank, 141–143
blood donation, 23, 92, 133, 142, 145–147
blood pressure measurement, 67–68
blood substitutes, 148
blood transfusions
  and disease transmission, 146–148
  hemolytic reaction, 93, 149
  immune reactions, 149–150, 180
  safety concerns, 148
  and surgery, 143
Blundell, James, 94
Bohr effect, 69

G

H

I